The Christian & War

The Christian & War

A Study That Asks Whether A Christian May
Scripturally Function As A Punitive Agent Of The
State And Other Related Questions

Allan Turner

ALLANITA PRESS
PUBLISHING

THE CHRISTIAN & WAR
© 2006 by Allan Turner

Published by Allanita Press

Cover design by Steve Sebree, Moonlight Graphics
Printed in the United States of America

ISBN 0-9777350-0-1

For information:
Allanita Press
4324A C.R. 200
Corinth, Mississippi 38834

Dedication

To all those true warriors, that "happy few," that "band of brothers,"* both secular and spiritual, who run toward, rather than from, the enemy's assault. May the God of heaven and earth, the One who is Himself a "man of war" (cf. Ex. 15:3), graciously bestow His blessings on all your noble deeds and self-sacrificing love, for "greater love has no one than this, than to lay down one's life for his friends" (Jn. 15:13).

> * "We few, we happy few, we band of brothers;
> For he to-day that sheds his blood with me
> Shall be my brother."
> —Shakespeare, *Henry V,* Act IV, Scene 3

Table of Contents

Preface

Since the Vietnam era, there has arisen, in America and the whole of Western society, a way of thinking that argues against all war. Consequently, a book discussing the question of a Christian's participation in war and other related issues in light of this emerging consensus seems not just appropriate but necessary.

The threat of world wars and global holocaust which loomed during the Cold War, although still quite possible today, seems to have dimmed with the passing of the twentieth century. Even so, some of the worst features of twentieth-century warfare continue to comprise our thinking about contemporary war-fighting. These have been articulated as:

> ...the understanding of war as an all-or-nothing conflict that can only end when one side is entirely victorious and the other entirely vanquished or driven into unconditional submission; the conception of the enemy as including all members of the opposing society, making a distinction between combatants and noncombatants irrelevant; the use of atrocity as a means of war; the use of ethnic, religious, or other cultural differences in much the same way as ideology was earlier employed to make the enemy appear less than human and, in any case, totally in the wrong.[1]

Thus, contemporary wars are still viewed within the framework of "total war" thinking—a way of thinking that views war as

---

[1] James Turner Johnson, *Morality And Contemporary Warfare*, 1999, p. 5.

immoral and therefore all war-fighting, even when deemed "necessary," as but a necessary evil.

In an environment where war is, by definition, immoral, it is difficult for "good," "decent" folks to think positively about war-fighting. This book is an effort to correct such thinking and to instruct the interested reader as to what the Bible actually says about this most important subject. Even so, there will always be Christians who, struggling with the complexities of what it means to be a true follower of Christ, will simply opt out of history and straightaway relinquish the business of government (which includes waging war, when necessary) to those who, all too frequently, have no overriding moral compunction to do what is right. Although this tradition has been well represented within Christendom, particularly among those who can be identified with the so-called Restoration Movement, I am convinced that such thinking was, from the beginning, and is, now, a terrible mistake that forces those who hold it to extend love to aggressors but not to their victims. Like the clergy of medieval days, these think the religion of Christ somehow lifts them above time, place and people. They think that Jesus' teachings, particularly those in the Sermon on the Mount, when coupled with His meek and humble life, effectively condemn the use of force and believe, I think quite erroneously, that the use of force is always wrong.

I have heard those who feel this way argue that although they believe the police-military power of the state is "necessary" to protect law-abiding citizens, they nevertheless believe all such "dirty hands" tasks should be carried out by worldly sinners, not Christians. These assert that there doesn't exist a governmental act involving the use of coercive, violent, or deadly force that does not demand repentance. Sin, they argue, is always committed when force is used, even when this force is implemented for just ends.

On the following pages, I will demonstrate why I believe such thinking to be not just wrongheaded, but completely unbiblical as well. No matter what your position may be on the subject of the Christian and war, you can expect to be challenged by what you will read here. Please know that it is my sincere desire not just to vindicate my point of view, although I will certainly be trying to do just that, but to ultimately glorify Jesus as the Lord of my life. I pray the Lord will bless you as you think about this subject in the light of His word.

Allan Turner
Corinth, Mississippi
April 2006

Chapter 1

The Opening Salvo

The pressing question at the beginning of this study is: *May a Christian scripturally function as a punitive agent of the state?* In answering this question, the Pacifist/Anti-War position responds with an emphatic "No!" The "My Country Right Or Wrong" position of unrestrained patriotism answers with an unqualified "Yes!" However, it has been my experience that simple answers rarely, if ever, do justice to complex questions. Therefore, the answers I will be giving to this and other questions during this study will be a bit more complex. After careful study, I hope you will find these answers to be honest, informative, and scriptural. But whether they are or not is a decision you'll have to make for yourself.

I will be arguing that (1) war is a moral enterprise, and (2) those who participate in it, if they do so justly, operate as servants of God and, as such, even in the extreme circumstances of war, stand before God's judgment and under His law. Unfortunately, these are ideas mostly lost on a culture consumed with the anti-war/pacifist consensus—a consensus that says war is always evil. Consequently, many Americans, and this includes more than a few Christians, view war as a conflagration of raw savagery to which no moral code applies. In other words, many believe that "War is Hell," as General William Tecumseh Sherman said in his attempt to justify the targeting of civilians in the Civil War siege and bombardment of Atlanta and his subsequent scorched-earth "march to the sea." Many today, like Sherman, see war as an evil, albeit a "necessary evil," that must, at times, be engaged in so worse evils are not inflicted. The General's concept of "Total War," as it has come to be known, eventually led to the direct targeting and bombing of civilians in World War II, including the ultimate decision to drop atomic bombs on the Japanese cities of Hiroshima and Nagasaki. In his justification for doing so, Truman said in an address to the American people on August 12, 1945:

> We have used [the bomb] against those who attacked us without warning at Pearl Harbor, against those who have starved and beaten and executed American prisoners of war, against those who have abandoned all pretense of obeying international laws of warfare. We have used it to shorten the agony of war...[1]

Yes, it seems that all Truman said about the Japanese was true, but it is interesting to note that Japan's attack on Pearl Harbor, although a dastardly deed, as Roosevelt called it, was directed entirely against naval and army installations, with only a few stray bombs falling on the city of Honolulu. Now, whether the Japanese military would have targeted our cities on the mainland, if they would have had the ability, is not doubted. Nevertheless, it disappoints me that our leaders, when they had the opportunity, did not take the moral high ground but, instead, *intentionally targeted civilians*, as did Sherman and others before them. But even prior to his decision to drop the atomic bombs, Truman, along with his advisors, had already bought into the "War is Hell" thinking, lock, stock and barrel. This is evidenced by the March 1945 fire-bombing of Tokyo in which incendiary bombs set off a firestorm that killed an estimated 100,000 people. As James Byrnes, Truman's good friend and Secretary of State, said, "...war remains what General Sherman said it was."[2] And Arthur Compton, who was chief scientific advisor to the government, confirmed this when he said, "...one realizes that in whatever manner it is fought, war is precisely what General Sherman called it."[3] Finally, in his own defense, Truman said, "Let us not become so preoccupied

---

[1] Michael Walzer, *Just And Unjust Wars: A Moral Argument With Historical Illustrations*, 1977, p. 264.

[2] Walzer, p. 265.

[3] *Ibid.*

with weapons that we lose sight of the fact that war itself is the real villain."[4]

So, to this way of thinking, wars, and not necessarily those who fight them, become the real villains. Therefore, it is then argued, any means to end a war, even when it involves incinerating hundreds of thousands of men, women, and children, becomes an unpleasant, but legitimate, tool. Such thinking led otherwise decent people, like Charles "Chuck" Yeager, to believe that once war is forced upon them, there are no limits, and therefore they are obligated to engage in any means, even atrocities, to end it. This is made clear from the following excerpt from Yeager's biography in which he describes a disturbing mission he was ordered to fly in World War II:

> Our seventy-five Mustangs were assigned an area fifty miles by fifty miles inside Germany and ordered to strafe anything that moved. The object was to demoralize the German population.... We weren't asked how we felt zapping people. It was a miserable, dirty mission, but we all took off on time and did it.... By definition, war is immoral; there is no such thing as a clean war. Once armies are engaged, war is total. We were ordered to commit an atrocity, pure and simple, but the brass who approved this action probably felt justified because wartime Germany was not easily divided between "innocent civilians" and its military machine.... In war, the military will seldom hesitate to hit civilians if they are in the way.... I'm certainly not proud of that particular strafing mission against civilians. But it is there, on the record and in my memory.[5]

Unfortunately, this kind of thinking did not stop with World War II. In defense of our nuclear strategy during the Cold War, General Omar Bradley argued that "war itself is immoral," and therefore in retaliation for attacks on our cities, it would be both

---

[4] *Ibid.*
[5] Chuck Yeager and Leo Janos, *Yeager*, 1985, p. 63.

moral and militarily useful to attack enemy cities.[6] And in response to the question of whether he had opposed the hydrogen bomb on moral grounds during hearings on J. Robert Oppenheimer, George Kenna, the former ambassador to what was then called the Soviet Union and a prominent Sovietologist, responded, "...I didn't consider that. After all, we are dealing with weapons here, and when you are dealing with weapons you are dealing with things that kill people, and I don't think the considerations of morality are relevant."[7]

Looking back on it now, it should not come as a surprise that such thinking led ultimately to the "search and destroy" tactics used by our military during the Vietnam War—tactics that caused our returning soldiers to be referred to by some as "baby killers." As much as it grieves me to say so, these charges were not totally unfounded. The "rules of engagement" in Vietnam were: (1) A village could be bombed or shelled without warning if American troops had received fire from within it; and (2) Any village known to be "hostile" could be bombed or shelled if its inhabitants were warned in advance, either by the dropping of leaflets or by helicopter loudspeakers.

Ironically, rules which were designed to separate noncombatants (civilians) from combatants (guerrillas) and therefore minimize casualties, actually provided the justification for attacking innocent men, women and children, as evidenced by the following incident which was typical in Vietnam—so typical, in fact, that it must have happened numerous times: "An American unit moving along Route 18 [in Long An province] received small arms fire from a village, and in reply the tactical commander called for artillery and air strikes on the village itself, resulting in heavy civilian casualties and extensive physical destruction."[8]

The policy underlying these rules of engagement (the so-called "pacification project") actually encompassed the uprooting and resettlement of a large number of the rural population in

---

[6] See Robert W. Tucker, *The Just War*, 1960, p. 59, note 52.

[7] Tucker, p. 77, note 70.

[8] Jeffery Race, *War Comes to Long An*, 1972, p. 233.

Vietnam: literally millions of men, women and children. Leaving aside the possible criminality of this project, it is safe to say that such uprooting and resettlement was, from its inception, simply an impossible task doomed for ultimate disaster—a disaster that caused, in the end, more violent death for Vietnamese civilians. Further, there never was more than a pretense that sufficient resources would be made available to accomplish the task. Therefore, it was inevitable that civilians would be living in the villages to be shelled and bombed. The following is an example of what happened:

> In August 1967, during Operation Benton, the "pacification" camps became so full that Army units were ordered not to "generate" any more refugees. The Army complied. But search and destroy operations continued. Only now the peasants were not warned before an air-strike was called on their village. They were killed in their villages because there was no room for them in the swamped pacification camps.[9]

Yes, war is hell, particularly when we feel justified in doing *whatever it takes* to win one. Whether we should have been in Vietnam in the first place is a debate that will, no doubt, continue to be hotly contested (I believe we had both the right and obligation to be there); but it is especially our conduct in prosecuting that war that is destined to remain a deep scar on the American conscience. The truth is that otherwise decent American soldiers did become baby killers, not because they wanted to, but because they thought they had to. We are, as a people, better than this, and if we cannot rise to a better standard, then no Christian can hope to serve this country without sin. Unless we are able to honestly consider where General Sherman's concept of "Total War" ultimately took us, then we will forever be torn between pacifism or the unrestrained patriotism of Total War. I believe there is a better way.

---

[9] Orville and Jonathan Shell, letter to *The New York Times*, Nov. 26, 1969; quoted in Noam Chomsky, *At War With Asia*, 1970, pp. 292-293.

No doubt, pacifists will argue that, writing as I have, I have already surrendered my position, providing *prima facie* evidence for why a Christian cannot, under any circumstances, participate in war; namely, that even among the best of governments there are a multitude of sinful acts that prove, conclusively, the "fallenness" of all civil governments. Therefore, these argue, a Christian, who is obligated to keep himself unspotted from the world,[10] cannot under any circumstances serve his government as a soldier without sinning. And if I held to the pacifist position, which says that any and all use of deadly force is inherently evil, I would be forced to recant my position. However, I do not believe any and all use of deadly force to be evil. On the contrary, I believe that to refrain from using such force, when justice demands it, would be the very thing that is inherently evil. That is, I believe that force, even when deadly, can be used justly and well in a good cause and that such acts bear no stain of evil.

At the same time, I readily admit that many, perhaps even most, of those who bear governmental authority are unworthy of it, stained openly, as they frequently are, with their own sin and crime. However, this reality does not negate their God-given responsibilities to protect the innocent and punish the evildoer. And therefore if fighting wars is part of the government's repertoire in these matters, and I will be arguing that it most certainly is, then governmental authorities are duty-bound (i.e., morally obligated), when justice demands it, to engage the enemy (foreign or domestic). When they do so, they operate as servants of the Most High God, the Ruler of the nations of the earth.

If our government has oppressed and abused other nations, then we ought to stop it, and those of us who are Christians ought to be praying God's mercy on our guilty country. But to argue, as some do, that our country can't now do what is right because of past failures is to advocate nothing short of dereliction of duty—a duty commanded by God. In point of fact, there is no coherent Biblical relationship between the acknowledgment of *past sins* and

---

[10] See Jas. 1:27.

the refusal of *present duty*. In other words, any government that today fails to safeguard its citizens because of past crimes will only be adding to its catalog of sins and, as such, will clearly be in neglect of its God-given responsibilities.[11]

Thankfully, the geopolitical experience that was Vietnam, a traumatic episode in our country's history that deeply wounded and splintered our nation, caused our government to stop and reflect on policies that had become divorced from the moral principles that ought to govern war—principles of which I'll have more to say as this study continues. Particularly, it learned that the public's perception of *how* a war is fought is as important as *why* it is fought. As a result, our government's renewed emphasis on accurate and precise targeting, along with a concerted effort to kill as few noncombatants as possible, and none intentionally, reflects a view of warfare that was manifested in the Gulf War (1990-91) and the current excursions in Afghanistan and Iraq. Although "collateral damage"[12] was an unfortunate reality in the Persian Gulf, Afghanistan and Iraq theaters, the small number of civilians killed was, and continues to be, absolutely amazing. These conflicts, at least on our side, represent the most cleanly fought modern wars on record and are more in line with the Just War principles developed down through the ages, particularly in Western civilization. I am delighted by this development and applaud those who have had a hand in causing it to happen, for without such an emerging consensus, I think there could be little hope of God's continued bountiful blessings upon our country, for as the Scriptures make abundantly clear, "Righteousness exalts a nation, but sin is a reproach to any people."[13]

I am not a warmonger, and will take umbrage to anyone who says I am. War must always be the last resort. This means if justice can be accomplished any other way, then war is not warranted. It should be clear from what I've said so far that I will not

---

[11] See Rom. 13:1-7.

[12] "Collateral damage" is the term the military uses to deal with the death and destruction of unintended targets.

[13] Prov. 14:34.

attempt to justify the evils that are all too frequently manifested in war. Nor will I defend, or in any way attempt to excuse, the unrestrained patriotism that always manifests itself when our country is threatened, as it now most certainly is. The state, even when it's the United States of America, is not superior to God's law. In fact, the state is what it is supposed to be *only* when it recognizes a Law above the law. Anything else is idolatry. The proof that the government of the United States of America views this principle correctly is manifested in the conscientious objector status it grants to its citizens who hold deeply felt, demonstrable, religious convictions that it would always be wrong to take human life, no matter what the circumstances.

In closing this introduction, I realize I haven't touched every nook and cranny of this issue. Even so, I hope I have whetted your appetite for a study of this most difficult and fundamentally important subject. It is to that study that I now direct your attention.

Chapter 2

What About The State's Role?

Contradicting General Sherman's "War is Hell" statement, Philip Lawler points out: "War is not hell. Hell is hell."[1] Commenting on this expression in the same book, Joseph P. Martino wrote:

> This is not just a witticism. Hell is the unrepentant sinner's final [punishment for] rejection of God, and God's eternal ratification of that rejection. The Christian who goes to war need not reject God. However, by waging war unjustly, he can do precisely that. War can become, then, not hell itself but the road to hell.[2]

Admittedly, the "war question," as it is sometimes called, is fraught with dangers. I'll be addressing some of these in this study. But before this can be done, the question of the State's right to wage war must be addressed. There are Christians who believe there is no such thing as a just war, and they are convinced that a Christian cannot participate in war-fighting without sinning. Romans 13:9 and 1 John 3:15, which *command* love and *prohibit* hate (and both in connection with murder and other such vices), have been cited by some as a refutation of all wars. In this chapter, I will try to demonstrate why such proof-texting is wrong.

Can a war be just? Yes, it can. How do I know? The Bible tells me so. In Romans 13:1-7, we have an inspired apostle's teaching on "conscientious citizenship," as some have described it, and I

---

[1] Quoted in Joseph P. Martino, *A Fighting Chance: The Moral Use of Nuclear Weapons*, 1988, p. 105.
[2] *Ibid.*

believe this is an apt description of what we find in these verses. But there is another side to this coin. While making it clear that citizens are obligated to submit to governing authorities, Paul gives us valuable and essential information concerning the government's responsibility to its citizens. In fact, these verses articulate the clearest teaching on the God-ordained purpose of human government to be found in the Bible. Thus, it is most unfortunate that some think Romans 13:1-7 to be incongruent with the immediate context of Romans 12:17-21, which says:

> Repay no one evil for evil. Have regard for good things in the sight of all men. If it is possible, as much as depends on you, live peaceably with all men. Beloved, do not avenge yourselves, but rather give place to wrath; for it is written, "Vengeance is Mine, I will repay," says the Lord. Therefore "If your enemy is hungry, feed him; if he is thirsty, give him a drink; for in so doing you will heap coals of fire on his head." Do not be overcome by evil, but overcome evil with good (NKJV).

The incongruists are wrong. Romans 13:1-7 explains (*amplifies* might be a better word) that while Christians are prohibited from executing personal vengeance, God has established civil government to be His earthly agent to see that such vengeance (i.e., justice) is meted out. Therefore, to teach Romans 12:17-21 without mentioning Romans 13:1-7 leaves not just a false impression as to what it means to be a Christian, but it fosters a lack of appreciation for the ministerial importance of civil government.

From these verses, it is reasonable to conclude that something God has ordained, like civil government and its right to use the sword, cannot be inherently evil, as some argue. Civil government, as articulated in Romans 13:1-7, is not evil, and those who participate in it do not sin when carrying out their God-ordained duties. Therefore, those who taint the God-given duties of civil government with sin are, whether they realize it or not, demonstrating opposition to that which God Himself has ordained. This makes the war issue not just a matter of personal scruples, as many claim, but of doctrine as well. But because brethren have danced around this issue for years in the name of peace and unity,

even squeezing it somehow into Romans 14, many have been influenced to think this subject "no big deal," and even if it is, it's
something which falls solely within the realm of personal ethics
and is, therefore, not something that should divide the church.
This is evidenced by the writings of Moses Lard, a distinguished
voice among 19th century disciples of Christ:

> To illustrate what I mean: it is held to be doubtful whether a Chris-
> tian man can go to war according to the New Testament. For myself
> I am candid to think he cannot. But others, let me allow, with equal
> candor think differently. Suppose now, we as a people, were equally
> divided on the point. Neither party could certainly force the other
> to accept its view. The difference should be held as a difference of
> opinion, and hence should be made a matter of forbearance. But
> should either party attempt to compel the other to accept its view,
> and in case of failure should separate, I should not hesitate to regard
> the separating party as a faction, and hence as condemned by the
> New Testament.[3]

Although Lard's position—not his position on pacifism, but division over the war issue—became the *de facto* position in many
churches of Christ, this was, in my opinion, most unfortunate.
Why? Because I believe the war issue, and how we deal with it, is
an extremely important issue that may very well determine where
we'll spend an eternity. But because we have largely dealt with
this issue using the Lard guidelines, many Christians have not seriously studied it and are, therefore, unable to decide, by faith,
whether or not a Christian is scripturally obligated to refrain from
all war-fighting. Of course, if pacifism is truly what being a follower of Christ requires, then it stands to reason that fellowship
cannot be extended to those who serve in the armed forces of our
country, for while military prowess may be the best assurance of
continued peace, it is clear that those who serve in the armed
forces of our country are not pacifists. Just such a view has been
expressed by a co-author of a recent debate on this subject:

---

[3] "Can We Divide?," *Lard's Quarterly III*, April 1866, pp. 331-332.

It should be noted that issues I am debating [have] always been a matter of faith with me ever since I became a Christian. That is, my beliefs are not so much based on personal qualms as they are on what the Bible reveals. I cannot but conclude that those who take my opponent's views on "just warfare," etc. are out of harmony with what God expects of [H]is people. Some may say that since my scruples do not concern the collective activity of Christians (such as using instrumental music in worship services would), I should be able to extend fellowship to those that disagree with me on the "civil government" issue. I beg to differ. To me, this is a moral issue that has bearing on the fate of people's souls just as other moral issues do (gambling, pornography, homosexuality, etc.). It is immaterial to me that many preachers have proverbially swept this issue under the rug, calling it a matter of "opinion." It is immaterial to me that many Christians do not share my views. What is important is what the Bible says about the matter.[4]

Integrity demands obedience to conscience, and I'm convinced that the brother mentioned above is just trying to do what he believes the Bible requires of him. Nevertheless, he and I are clearly on divergent paths, and so much so that if we were in the same congregation we'd have serious issues of fellowship to contend with. However, although our divergent views ultimately produce questions of fellowship, fellowship, *per se*, is not the issue before us. Such can be hashed out later, if the need arises. At issue *now* is what the Bible teaches on the government's and Christian's role in war. Even so, when what we believe affects how others perceive us (viz., good, bad, brave, cowardly, foolish, wise, consistent, inconsistent, orthodox, heterodox, *et cetera*), caution and soft-speaking should be the order of the day. So although I will be pressing my points firmly and, I hope, succinctly, it must not be thought that I am shouting and snorting condemnation at those who disagree with me on this subject. In fact, as long as a pacifist is content to have fellowship with me, I would not advocate, nor would I ever initiate, withdrawing from him. Yes, I do believe the

---

4 Reference citation to this 1998 debate not given to protect the guilty.

pacifist needs to change his position, and I will be praying for just that, and that this study will advance that end.

At the same time, I admit I could be wrong and in need of repentance myself. If I am, I would appreciate very much being corrected. Consequently, I look forward to hearing from those with opposing views. And although I am optimistic that good can be accomplished by such an exchange, I nevertheless remain convinced there will always be Christians who, struggling with the complexities of what it means to be a true follower of Christ, will simply opt out of history and summarily relinquish the business of government to those who all too often have no conscientious scruples at all. This tradition, as I've already pointed out, has been well represented in churches of Christ. I am convinced that such thinking was, from the beginning, and is now, a terrible mistake that forces the one who holds it to extend love to aggressors but not to their victims. This, to me, is a critical point, and I'll have more to say about it as this study progresses.

My Position Clearly Stated

Personally, I would be overjoyed if every government official was a Christian. And if every policeman and soldier were a Christian, is there anyone who would not think we'd be much better off? However, in affirming a Christian's right (and sometimes duty) to participate in the use of armed force, whether as a policeman or soldier, I do not intend to defend, nor excuse, all that professed Christians have done in these positions. Indeed, not all wars are moral, and therefore it would be wrong (i.e., unjust) for a Christian to participate in such. Secondly, although some wars are moral (i.e., just), and therefore permissible for Christians to participate in, I believe certain moral restrictions must always apply to the fighting of such wars. Thus, a Christian who participates in a just war is not immune from the moral obligations that bear on his conduct. I tried to make this clear in the introduction, and I mention it here again only because pacifists all too frequently misunderstand my position, preferring to identify it as one that justifies killing anyone my government mandates. This may be a correct description of one who believes it is always right to participate in war (i.e., "activism"[5]), but for me, a selective conscientious objector (i.e., "selectivism"[6]), I categorically deny that mine is such a position. Selectivism rests uneasily between the activism that shouts, "My country, right or wrong!," and the pacifism that would permit a Hitler or Saddam Hussein to commit genocide without lifting a weapon in resistance. Having reiterated this, it is time for us to turn our attention to the task at hand.

The Sword

Down through the centuries, most non-Christians have equated Christianity with pacifism. This is understandable, as most non-believers are hardly qualified to be exegetes of the New Testament. But it is most unfortunate that one claiming to be a New Testament Christian would think so, for such thinking has caused many to think of Christianity as "an ideal and beautiful religion" that is impractical except for a few rare individuals (viz., pacifists). This false image leads to high-sounding principles that are, after all is said and done, impossible to keep in practice. The world is fallen and full of evil, therefore, Jesus, many think, demands that which is impossible. Thus, unless the "impossibilism" of Christ is replaced with the "possibilism" of politics (for politics, if it is anything, is certainly the art of the possible), then civilizations are destined to be overrun by tyrants and despots. Such thinking has caused many people to be corrupted, producing at least two types of individuals: (1) those who, although they profess Christianity, will not act according to its *real* and *practical* tenets, which make a distinction between the shedding of innocent blood and the shedding of any human blood, and (2) those who, although they profess nominal Christianity, would never act on what they consider to be its *false* and *impracticable* tenets, particularly the supposed tenet of pacifism. Both groups, convinced that a number

---

[5] The *activist* has no qualms about participating in carnal warfare. He believes any time his country ask him to fight, he is obligated to do so.

[6] The *selectivist* believes there are times when he would not be able to fight for his country. However, if the war is just, he believes he could do so without sin.

of things are wicked which are not, and seeing no way to avoid wickedness being done in a fallen world, ultimately partake of a dialogue that sets no limits on warfare.

However, New Testament Christianity, contrary to the false image of "pacifistic Christianity," is quite practical. Because it is, God has given the state the awesome responsibility of using the sword to restrain, punish and, when necessary, kill evildoers.[7] Why? Because, although the Bible prohibits individuals from exercising revenge or vengeance,[8] civil government was ordained by God for this very purpose.[9] I honestly do not see how it is possible for anyone who is a Christian to misunderstand this point. Therefore, when officials of the state duly carry out their responsibilities to do good toward the law-abiding and visit wrath (i.e., punishment) on those who do evil, it is hard for me to understand how some Christians think this to be a task only for the unregenerated. On the contrary, God calls these civil authorities His *ministers* who are to be "attending continually to this very thing."[10] How then can anyone be sinning by doing what God appointed him to do? Frankly, I don't think there's a pacifist answer to this question that is anywhere close to being Scriptural. Nevertheless, some have cited God's use of evil nations to punish other evil nations as an answer. But God's use of an evil nation, which got that way by its own volition, to punish another evil nation is in no way parallel to the situation under discussion, and I fail to see how anyone but those grasping for straws could not understand this.

Therefore, the state, when acting in accordance with the Law above the law, is authorized to take human life for the good of those it has been ordained to protect and the punishment of those who do evil. Such God-ordained taking of life, although it may certainly be described as killing, is not, as some think, unlawful killing or murder. Consequently, an official of the state cannot be sinning when he carries out this morally constituted duty, and

---

[7] See Rom. 13:1-7.
[8] See Rom. 12:17-21.
[9] See Rom. 13:4.
[10] Rom. 13:6; see also verse 4.

those who so argue are *clearly* (and by this term I mean *unequivocally*) in violation of God's prohibition against calling good evil and evil good.[11] So, before we even get to the question of whether a Christian can scripturally engage in carnal warfare, the pacifists, who believe that any such lawful use of the sword is, in point of fact, murder, has some backing up to do. If one can't get this issue right, then I fail to see how he could ever be convinced from the Scriptures that a Christian has a right, and sometimes a duty, under certain circumstances, to participate in carnal warfare. Nevertheless, it is to this issue I now direct your attention.

Living What We Believe And Vice Versa

God never calls upon Christians to do what is impossible, impractical or unlivable. In fact, one of the strongest proofs of the validity of Christianity is that we can *live what we believe* and *believe what we live*. As a Christian, I cannot take vengeance into my own hands (I'm speaking here as an individual). To do so would be a sin. [12] But such a moral code does not make me, as a Christian and law-abiding citizen, prey and fodder for evildoers. Why? Because ever since sin entered into the world, God has understood His people would be living in a world where evildoers would want to harm and take advantage of the law-abiding. Knowing that when left to our own devices we might be tempted to return evil for evil, bitterness for bitterness, gossip for gossip, slander for slander, hatred for hatred, *et cetera*, God ordained civil government as a mechanical remedy against unrestrained evil. In doing so, He stated that anyone who sheds man's blood (i.e., commits murder) by man shall his blood be shed.[13] Notice, if you will, that this verse condemns the *wrongful* taking of human life as well as authorizes the *rightful* taking of human life. Further note that this verse is not an "Old Testament" ordinance, *per se*; instead, it is God's law for all mankind for all time, enforceable before, during and after the

---

[11] See Isa. 5:20.
[12] See Rom. 12:19.
[13] That is, would receive capital punishment (cf. Genesis 9:6).

law of Moses. If this is true, and I don't see how anyone can deny it, then we would expect to see this ordinance incorporated into both the Old and New Covenants, and this is, of course, exactly what we find.[14]

Israel, under the law of Moses, was a theocracy. As such, it was at times directly guided into war by God. Although these occasions can be used to demonstrate that God is not anti-war, *per se*, nevertheless, the United States of America is not a theocracy. Therefore, I will concede that it can be argued that what applied *uniquely* to Israel as God's chosen instrument is not *normative* for any other nation. But in doing so, I will not give up the fact that Jehovah, according to Exodus 15:3, is a "man of war" or "warrior," depending on what translation one is using. Furthermore, one can be sure that the Bible's prohibition against murder was not transgressed by Israel when they were led into war by God. Therefore, it is clear, once again, that not all killing is murder. If one understands this, then progress is being made.

Additionally, the Bible makes it clear that God did not consider killing in self-defense to be murder. In Exodus 22:2, Moses said, "If the thief is found breaking in, and he is struck so that he dies, there shall be no guilt for his bloodshed." Such rests upon the probability that those who break in at night[15] may very well have murderous intent, and that when discovered would, in order to escape, be predisposed to commit murder. Why then would anyone but a committed pacifist think that this principle—a principle which would later be incorporated into Roman, English and American law—would not also be in force under the New Covenant?

What's more, Genesis 14 is an example[16] of God's approval of Abraham's war against the kings of the valley. This can be seen by Melchizedek's blessing of Abraham after he had attacked and routed his foreign enemies:

---

[14] See Ex. 20:13; Rom. 13:9.
[15] See the very next verse.
[16] During the Patriarchal dispensation.

Then Melchizedek king of Salem brought out bread and wine; he was the priest of God Most High. And he blessed him and said: "Blessed be Abram of God Most High, Possessor of heaven and earth; and blessed be God Most High, Who has delivered your enemies into your hand." And he [Abraham] gave him a tithe of all.[17]

This divinely sanctioned war is particularly important in that it occurred before Israel was established as a theocracy.[18] Therefore, it cannot be argued that this is a special case of theocratic warfare. If not, and if what was written in Genesis 14:18-20 was written for our learning,[19] then why would anyone think such actions (i.e., the active doing of justice) to be wrong under the New Covenant? In fact, the New Testament continues to affirm that deadly force (i.e., the sword) is still a divinely ordained means of executing human justice. Writing of the civil authorities, Paul said, "For he is God's minister to you for good. But if you do evil, be afraid; for he does not bear the sword in vain; for he is God's minister, an avenger to execute wrath on him who practices evil."[20]

The New Testament's Teaching On The Separation Of Church And State

When it comes to the New Testament, the Lord made it clear there would be a separation between *Church* (viz., spiritual Israel) and *State*.[21] Under this system, the sword was granted to the State, not the Church.[22] Therefore, Christians, engaged as they are in spiritual warfare, do not fight with carnal weapons.[23] This simply means that all the "holy wars," past, present and future,

---

[17] Gen. 14:18-20.
[18] See Ex. 19.
[19] See Rom. 15:3.
[20] Rom. 13:4.
[21] See Matt. 22:21.
[22] Rom. 13:4.
[23] See 2 Cor. 10:4.

were not, and cannot be, pleasing to God. The borders of God's kingdom are not advanced by armed force.

On the other hand, the state is duly authorized by God to advance its cause by force of arms. In doing so, it is under obligation to defend its citizens from enemies (i.e., evildoers), both foreign and domestic. Although Romans 13:1-7 appears on the surface to deal specifically with domestic law enforcement, it certainly seems to be faulty logic to argue, as some do, that the state may use armed force to protect its citizens from a murderous individual while, at the same time, it must let a murderous country run roughshod over thousands, even millions, of innocent people. No, no, no, a thousand times, no! The state's authority to "bear not the sword in vain" implies the right to use deadly force to restrain and punish evildoers, whether they be domestic or foreign. In fact, the distinction between soldier and policeman is a rather recent invention. It was the armed legions of Rome that fought its wars and kept the peace. The enforcement of the law, the maintenance of order, and the protection of the innocent, which today are the province of the police, were in Paul's day the responsibility of soldiers. How then can anyone doubt that the sword in the hand of a civil magistrate represented both the military and law enforcement obligations the state owed its citizenry?

Consequently, and I believe most reasonable exegetes will agree, the state's God-given authority to administer justice, by reason of legitimate extrapolation, includes the restraint of and resistance to evildoers who are aggressors as well as those who are criminals, and therefore requires the State to protect its citizens' rights when threatened from outside as well as from within.

Finally, to deny, on moral grounds, the elementary right of the state to defend itself and its citizens by war simply means to deny the legitimate existence of the state itself, which would be, in turn, contrary to the Scriptures.

The Restraints Of War

Presently, George W. Bush, as President, is the executive head of our government. This means he is commander-in-chief of the Armed Forces. Thus, when the citizens of this nation are threatened by foreign forces, as they now are, Mr. Bush is acting within his God-given duty to execute wrath on the evildoers who have targeted not just our soldiers, but innocent men, women and children as well. He has said the U.S. will either bring these aggressors to justice or justice to these aggressors. This is executive justice and it is just the kind of justice in view in Romans 13:4. Such justice, whether in connection with crime, civil disorder, or international warfare, must be *discriminate* (i.e., limited to the evildoers and those who support them) and *controlled* (i.e., limited only to the force necessary to secure such justice). This brings us necessarily to an examination of the Just War tradition.

The Virtues Of War

The Just War tradition that has developed in the West has been amplified by the works of Ambrose, Augustine, Aquinas, Luther, Zwigli, Calvin, *et al.*, but if it is to have any real meaning for New Testament Christians, it must be because such a tradition is, first and foremost, grounded in the Bible. The think-sos of men can be interesting and even informative, but they are not authoritative. Hence, I do not feel obligated to affirm every nuance of the Just War tradition articulated in the past or today. On the other hand, the Christian is obligated to apply the New Testament to everything he does in this world, and this includes not only his obligation to the Church, but also the State. Thus, it is to the New Testament and its principles that the child of God must look to find the virtues, if any, of warfare.

As I've tried to make clear, a major key to understanding the Just War tradition is to be found in the New Testament's teaching concerning the purpose of government.[24] As we learned, the main purpose of government is to promote, preserve and enforce *justice*. By now it ought to be clear that there are two major aspects of justice. One is distributive justice, which includes protecting the rights of the innocent, and involves the right to life and the right

---

[24] See Rom. 13:1-7.

to be free from oppression.[25] The other is *retributive* justice, which involves the just punishment of those who deserve it due to their trampling on the rights of others. The Bible teaches us unequivocally that killing is permissible as an act of retributive justice.[26] Therefore, murder is *wrong* because it is the taking of *innocent* life, and capital punishment is *right* because it is *just retribution* against a murderer. Clearly, most wars follow this pattern. When one nation launches an attack against another, bent on conquest, pillage and destruction, it incurs guilt in the same way a murderer does, albeit on a much larger scale. This means that individual soldiers engaging in acts of aggression share in this guilt and are, therefore, subject to death in the interest of retributive justice. Thus, the attacked nation is morally right when it kills guilty aggressors, as such is the moral equivalence of capital punishment.

However, the main consideration when it comes to warfare is *not* retributive, but *distributive*, justice, which is, after all, the primary purpose of government ordained by God. A Romans 13 government[27] will do its level best to serve and protect its citizens. Specifically, this involves providing them with a just, free, and peaceable environment. Such a government will protect its citizens from acts of injustice, whether committed by individual criminals or aggressive nations, and the justice God requires demands it. Pacifism's "peace at any price" is not a Biblical position. Refusing to take human life when justice demands it, as the pacifist does, is a perversion not just of justice itself, but the Scriptures that demand it. Consequently, *pacifism* is not the answer. But, as we've already argued, neither is *activism's* "My country, right or wrong," "I'll kill 'um if my country asks me to." This means it's up to *selectivists*, who think the *why* and *how* of war must be just, to set the ground rules for appropriate war-fighting.

---

[25] See I Tim. 2:1-4.

[26] See Gen. 9:6 and Rom. 13:1-7.

[27] Namely, a God-fearing government that occupies itself with upholding justice and righteousness.

The Rules Of A Just War

Space does not permit a lengthy dissertation on Just War doctrine. However, I do find it necessary to mention the basic components or categories that all Just War advocates agree upon. The first of these, *jus ad bellum*,[28] has to do with *the reasons* that justify going to war. The second, *jus in bello*,[29] with *how* a just war is to be conducted.

The Reasons For War

In order to be just, a war must be defensive. As such, its aim is to protect the innocent from unjust aggression. Further, it must be undertaken with the right intention, which is to restore a just peace. When such a war is decided upon, it must be with an understanding that the means used will be proportionate to the ends sought. In addition, a just war can be engaged in only when it has been reasonably determined that there are no viable alternatives for resolving the conflict. Finally, to meet a Just War criteria, there must be a reasonable probability of success in achieving the aims of the war. This very briefly describes the *jus ad bellum* criteria that must be present before one can engage in fighting a just war.

Conduct In War

The second category, *jus in bello*, which has to do with "the how" (or conduct) of a just war is quite distinct, and must be kept so. The various nuances of this category can be many, but the criteria are essentially two: *proportionality* and *discrimination*.

The first, proportionality, has to do with using only the force necessary to effect the desired results. In other words, to vindicate

---

[28] *Jus ad bellum* is a Latin term that deals primarily with the idea that in order to be just, there are certain conditions that must be met before a resort to war can be justified.

[29] *Jus in bello* is a Latin term that argues that once a just war is undertaken, it must be waged justly.

a just cause, no more force than is necessary can be resorted to. Consequently, the disproportionate use of force is not only inappropriate, but wrong (i.e. "evil"), and thus punishable by law.

The second, discrimination, is also called "noncombatant immunity," and has to do with the idea that there must be no intentional killing of innocent civilians. In modern parlance, this has come to be called "collateral damage," a term I'm not all that pleased with, as it can detract from the fact that innocent civilians have been killed. However, in defense of the term, it must be pointed out that those using it are doing so to make it clear that they have not purposefully targeted innocent civilians, which is the exact opposite of what the September 11th, 2001 attacks on America did. This naturally brings us to the current war on terrorism and the question of whether or not it meets Just War criteria.

I answer the above question with an unequivocal "Yes." I do so because the war on terror meets all the criteria of the Just War principles outlined above. Because our government has (1) the right authority, (2) a just cause and (3) the right intention, I believe the present war against Muslim *jihadis*,[30] and those who support them, is not just right, but obligatory. Therefore, for me to fail to lend my support to its efforts would be a failure of virtue—that is, a failure to act consistently with the principles of Righteousness and Justice taught in God's Word. Conjointly, I believe if I were to fail (as all genuine pacifists must do) to lend my support to this war, I would be doing a terribly vicious thing, in that I would be failing to show charity (i.e., love) toward my neighbor and, thus, toward God.[31] Because charity forms the foundation for the "good works" I believe I was "created in Christ Jesus" to do,[32] I sincerely pray that I will be willing, like the many before me, to lay down my life, when necessary, for my neighbor. If this isn't to be included in the "pure and undefiled religion" that

---

[30] This is the plural form of *jihadi*: one who engages in Islamic *Jihad* or "Holy War."

[31] See Lk. 10:27.

[32] See Eph. 2:10.

Christians are to practice,[33] then I fail to see how anything else could.

In the next chapter, we'll examine more closely the Christian's role in just warfare.

---

[33] See Jas. 1:27.

Chapter 3

What About The Christian's Role?

Although Christians are prohibited from taking personal vengeance, God has provided a remedy to protect not just Christians, but all law-abiding citizens from those who would do them harm. This remedy is civil government. It is most unfortunate that pacifists, like the clergy of medieval days, think the religion of Christ somehow lifts them above *time*, *place* and *people*. They think Jesus' teachings—particularly those in the Sermon on the Mount, coupled with His meek and humble life—effectively condemn the use of force, and that it is, therefore, *always wrong*.

I have heard some of them argue that although they believe the police-military power of the state is "necessary" to protect law-abiding citizens, they nevertheless believe all such "dirty hands" tasks should be carried out by sinners, not Christians. This seems awfully condescending. According to these Christian elitists, there does not exist a governmental act involving the use of coercive, violent or deadly force that does not demand repentance. Sin, they argue, is always committed when force is used, even when this force is implemented for just ends. I believe I have demonstrated such thinking to be not just wrongheaded, but unscriptural as well. So in this chapter I want to examine the role Christians may play in just wars.

While a Christian (pacifist or otherwise) may not be able to picture Jesus—whose unique work was grounded in the priestly role of reconciliation and intercession—as a soldier or policeman, it should not be so hard for someone to understand how a soldier or policeman, who is primarily motivated by charity (and I'm talking about the love of God and neighbor here), would be conscience driven to do all he could to restrain evil so that justice could be done. In other words, the question is not what would Jesus do?, but what would Jesus have us to do?

Service Motivated By Love

Nevertheless, such strikes a discordant note for many Christians. "How," they ask, "can force, deadly or otherwise, be loving?" In short, it can't unless it seeks to mimic God's use of force. This means, among other things, that the *just* use of force can never involve intrinsic evil.[1] Armed force is charity, then, only when it seeks to resemble God's use of force.

Pacifists frequently argue that the commandment to love one's enemies prohibits the Christian, as an official of government, from exercising deadly force. "After all," they ask, "if one truly loves his enemy, how can he shoot him?" Well, when his enemy has surrendered, he can't! When his enemy is defenseless, he can't! In fact, there are a multitude of reasons why a Christian functioning as a soldier would not shoot his enemy, and this has frequently been the difference between the actions of armies reflecting Biblical-based ethics and those that don't. As I write this, sworn enemies of the United States are being provided special food consistent with their religious beliefs, adequate shelter, and medical treatment far superior to what they would receive in their own countries, and all at taxpayers' expense. To me, this sounds much like the Biblical injunction to return good for evil.[2]

But let me ask a few questions that may help us focus our attention: Did God cease loving mankind when He destroyed all but eight souls in a worldwide flood? Does the fact that many will be punished for an eternity in a Devil's hell mean that God does not love every human being, even to the point of sending His own Son into this world to die for him? Well, if God can love His enemies but still punish them, why can't we?

---

[1] The *intentional* killing of innocent people would be intrinsic evil.
[2] See Rom. 12:21; 1 Thess. 5:15.

Yes, we are called upon to love our enemies, and we must do so, but, and this is often overlooked by pacifists, the Christian is also obligated to love the innocent citizens who stand to be enslaved or murdered by an attacking army. What then is love's responsibility to them? Is it not to seek distributive justice? Is it not to defend their God-given rights? Clearly, love's responsibility to protect the innocent must prevail. Thus, I conclude that a just war may be engaged in not only to see that justice is done, but to demonstrate love itself. Contrary to the think-sos of pacifists, God does not believe in, nor does the Bible teach, "peace at any price." Refusing to restrain an evildoer, or when necessary to take his life, when justice and love demand it, is a gross distortion of New Testament Christianity.

God has made it clear that He desires to restrain evil among His creatures. To do so, He has authorized the use, when necessary, of deadly force. This is, as we've learned, the primary purpose of God-ordained[3] governments, and those who righteously attend such governments are called nothing less than *ministers of God for good*.[4] With this in mind, it is important to note what God said through the prophet in Isaiah 5:20-21:

> Woe to those who call evil good, and good evil; Who put darkness for light, and light for darkness; who put bitter for sweet, and sweet for bitter! Woe to those who are wise in their own eyes, and prudent in their own sight!

Consequently, when Christian pacifists argue it is wrong (viz., that it is "evil") for Christians to serve as "God's minister to you for good," why should they not be seen as those who come under the condemnation of calling good evil, and evil good?

But there is more. In Jesus' condemnation of those who were willing, as a result of their misinterpretation/misapplication of Scripture, to condemn the guiltless, He said, "But if you had

---

[3] See again Rom. 13.
[4] See Rom. 13:4,6; 1 Pet. 2:14.

known what this means, 'I desire mercy and not sacrifice,' you would not have condemned the guiltless."[5] In other words, Jesus is saying that when His disciples acted as they did, they acted consistent with principles taught in His Word. Therefore, it should be clear His disciples did not break God's law, as they were being wrongly accused of doing by a bunch of haughty, self-righteous, and hypocritical religionists. If Jesus' encounters with these people sound a bit harsh, be assured they were. Jesus was not being "nice," as most people today count "niceness." Instead, He was "contentious" about what He was saying, for He was addressing an issue that would ultimately determine where human beings created in His image would spend an eternity. He advanced this same theme in Matthew 23:23-24, where He said:

> Woe to you, scribes and Pharisees, hypocrites! For you pay tithe of mint and anise and cummin, and have neglected the weightier matters of the law: justice and mercy and faith. These you ought to have done, without leaving the others undone. Blind guides, who strain out a gnat and swallow a camel!

Because *justice, mercy* and *faith* were important ideas to Jesus, it behooves every Christian to spend some time contemplating these "weightier matters of the law," particularly as they relate to the issue at hand.

The Weightier Matters

The Christian can be sure that the kind of "faith" Jesus was talking about in the passage above is not merely mental assent. It is, instead, the *saving faith* manifested by works[6]—works, I might add, of *mercy* and *justice*. In answering the question of whether or not a man can be saved by faith *alone*, James said it this way:

---

[5] Matt. 12:7
[6] See Jas. 2:14-26.

If a brother or sister is naked and destitute of daily food, and one of you says to them, "Depart in peace, be warmed and filled," but you do not give them the things which are needed for the body, what does it profit? Thus also faith by itself, if it does not have works, is dead. But someone will say, "You have faith, and I have works." Show me your faith without your works, and I will show you my faith by my works.[7]

Suppose, then, that a little old lady walking to the market is attacked by thugs who have knocked her to the ground in an effort to steal her purse. Suppose that because that purse contains all the money she has, and because it's just enough to get her through another week, she momentarily hesitates to let go of it. Suppose, in their efforts to make her let go of the purse, one of the thugs begins to kick her in the side, while yet another tries to break her arm in an effort to make her let go. Is she acting ungodly by trying to protect her livelihood? Now, suppose you are a witness to this whole thing. Do you mean to tell me that the principles of justice, righteousness and mercy require you to do nothing more than yell for someone who is a "sinner anyway" to come and stop these vicious criminals? What kind of faith would this be? And what kind of pathetic religion is it that would seek to brand this old lady a sinner for resisting her attackers and who, in order to be helped, needs sinners[8] to be called in order to do what is right? Those who practice such a creed and, in turn, look down their noses at those of us they call "carnal Christians" must, I think, be identified with the scribes and Pharisees of Jesus' day who, although they claimed *élitist* positions in their service to God, had neglected the weightier matters of the law.

---

[7] Jas. 2:15-18.
[8] Namely, the alleged "unrighteous servants" of the government.

But How About Not Returning Evil For Evil?

Yes, the Bible does talk about not returning evil for evil,[9] but unless one's conscience condemns him,[10] *it is never evil to do what is right*. In fact, the Bible says, "He who practices righteousness is righteous."[11] So, even though sentiment has now evolved to the point that many believe it is wrong (i.e., "evil") to inflict corporal punishment, even on one's own children, and even though this sentiment is now being enforced by law in some places, God caused it to be recorded long ago that "He who spares his rod hates his son, but he who loves him disciplines him promptly."[12] The Bible makes it clear that even God provides such chastening to His own children.[13] Consequently, when a child does wrong and is properly punished for it, such is *not an evil* to be eradicated, *but a virtue* to be upheld. Along these same lines, when policemen and soldiers put their lives on the line in order to *serve* their fellow citizens and *protect* them from evil, they are involved in the highest form of love the Bible commands—the self-sacrificing love that is willing, if necessary, to lay its life down for another.[14] This remains true even when such love includes the deadly, but just, use of force. Therefore, the Scriptural prohibition against returning evil for evil has nothing to do with the legitimate, lawful, and righteous utilization of force, for "Against such there is no law."[15]—never has been, and never will be!

But How About Turning The Other Cheek?

Yes, when giving instructions regarding *personal* ethics, Jesus talked about turning the other cheek. He did so in the context of not resisting an evil person, nor invoking the "eye for eye and

---

9 See Rom. 12:17; I Thess. 5:15; I Pet. 3:9.

10 See Rom. 14:23.

11 I Jn. 3:7.

12 Prov. 13:24, see also 19:18.

13 See 2 Sam. 7:14; Heb. 12:5-11; Rev. 3:19.

14 See Rom. 5:6-10.

15 Gal. 5:23b.

tooth for tooth" mandate of the Mosaical Law in some exercise of personal revenge.[16] Therefore, it ought to be abundantly clear that He was not addressing His remarks to civil authorities, who He had authorized to exercise just such vengeance and punishment. Instead, He was addressing the common man and was, therefore, dealing *only* with personal ethics. On the other hand, if it is true that the turning-the-other-cheek mandate was a New Testament principle to be applied across the board to individuals and governments, as many pacifists claim, then the apostle Paul definitely got it wrong in Romans 13:1-7. This would be an argument that the Bible actually contradicts itself; but what Christian is willing to believe such a thing? Incidentally, many have thought the ethics taught by Jesus here in these "turn the other cheek" verses, although laudable, are not attainable in a fallen world. Consequently, they have believed them to be something destined for implementation in a yet future millennial kingdom. This is a mistake. Jesus' instructions here, although extremely difficult, are the most practical ever given to man. The individual who understands and implements this personal set of ethics will learn to cultivate the kind of life God created mankind to live from the very beginning.

Further, and this point must not be missed, there was absolutely nothing wrong with the *lex talionis*[17] principle taught in the law of Moses. In fact, it was, and still is, the model *par excellence* for earthly justice. However, *lex talionis* was not created as a personal set of ethics. It was, instead, created as a judicial remedy against the personal vengeance that seldom manifests the weightier matters of the law—things like justice, mercy and faith. However, if all mankind were to live according to the principles articulated in the Sermon on the Mount, there would be no need for the mechanical remedies provided by civil authorities. But because mankind is fallen, Romans 13 governments, which are governments ordained by God, function as God-given ministers of

---

[16] See Matt. 5:38-39; Ex. 21:24.

[17] *Lex talionis* is a Latin term encompassing the law of like for like, that is, eye for eye, tooth for tooth, burning for burning, *et cetera*.

Justice and Righteousness. Governmental authorities, even when they fail to realize it, and whether they like it or not, are subject to Christ's Law above the law and will answer to His "rod of iron" if their policies are contrary to His principles.[18] The degree to which a government finds this offensive is a good indicator of just how far down the path towards a Revelation 13 government[19] it has traveled.

The Need For Salty Christians

"Righteousness exalts a nation; but sin is a reproach to any people."[20] There are more New Testament Christians in America than any place else in the world, and these, I am convinced, function as the salt that continues to preserve this nation.[21] Therefore, the righteous acts of Christians are not only important to the salvation of Christians themselves, but to the preservation of our nation as well. If our government, God forbid, ever becomes a full-fledged Revelation 13 government, openly and deliberately persecuting God's people, it will go down to the pit, as did the Roman Empire. Any nation that messes with God's people makes itself an enemy of God, and the enemies of God do not prevail. Nevertheless, and in the meantime, the godly salt of faithful Christians continues to preserve our great nation.

But consider a most sobering thought: What happens when this salt loses its savor? Jesus said it would be good for nothing but to be cast out and trodden under the foot of men.[22]

To permit a murder to occur when it could have been prevented is morally wrong. To allow a rape when one could have deterred it is an evil, not a good, as the pacifists must argue. To watch an act of cruel abuse of a child without stepping in to end it is morally

---

[18] See Psa. 2:9; Rev. 2:27; 12:5; 19:15.

[19] A Rev. 13 government is a government ordained by Satan and under his sway.

[20] Prov. 14:34.

[21] See Matt. 5:13.

[22] *Ibid.*

inexcusable. What's more, to call such intercession evil, and not good, is itself evil and does not reflect the rightly divided principles taught in the Bible. The word of God says, "Anyone, then, who knows the right thing to do and fails to do it, commits sin."[23] In other words, not properly resisting evil is a *sin of omission*, which can be just as evil as a *sin of commission*. A man who will not protect his wife and children against a violent intruder, even when he believes the Bible prohibits him from doing so, fails them miserably. And although it is true a pacifist who rightly defended his wife and children would sin by doing so, in that he would be violating his own conscience,[24] he would, nevertheless, be sinning if he did not. Therefore, the pacifist's "damned if you do; damned if you don't" dilemma should serve to demonstrate the importance of getting this issue right. Happily, God's word, when properly interpreted, does not create such dilemmas.

Likewise, any government that has the means to defend its citizens against a foreign aggressor and fails to do so is morally delinquent. Even as justice demands a life for a life in capital crimes, the same logic can be extended to the unjust actions of nations, and this means that a nation has a moral duty to take punitive actions against an aggressor nation, with Hilter being a case in point. It would have been morally wrong for the Allied forces (in this case a group of aggrieved nations) not to resist Nazi Germany. Even so, the Christian pacifist argues the New Testament is silent on war and international justice, in that Romans 13:1-7 deals only with citizens' obligation to government and the government's responsibility to its citizens. Yes, it is true that Romans 13:1-7 is specifically addressing domestic citizen-government responsibilities and obligations. But I've argued, and I think correctly so, that the demands of justice God has placed on government obviously project these same principles to matters involving international justice. And to not do so would be convoluted, to say the least, for it would require a nation to serve and protect its citizens from

---

[23] Jam. 4:17, NRSV.
[24] See Rom. 14:22-23.

domestic evildoers, but not from the aggression and violence of foreign tyrants.

So, instead of making the government's work harder by attempting to prohibit its God-given right to use deadly force, Christians should be willing to uphold the government's righteous hand as it does justice.[25] Admittedly, and even understandably, not every Christian is suitable for military or police service. But for a New Testament Christian to look down his nose at fellow Christians who serve their fellow citizens in this fashion is, in my opinion, unthinkably obtuse. I have discussed, argued with, and even been cajoled by, brethren who charge that a Christian cannot, as they like to put it, "kill for his government" without committing sin. I've even known of congregations where some wanted to refuse the Lord's Supper to our men and women in uniform, particularly those serving in our Armed Forces. Understanding, as I do, that a Christian cannot violate his conscience without committing sin, I respect, and will even defend, a Christian's decision to be a "conscientious objector." But I think any such Christian needs to be extremely careful in his or her condemnation of those of us who believe that not only can we use deadly force to protect the innocent, but that, in some cases, we *must* do so if we are not to be counted as sinners. One such fellow, a preacher of the gospel, made it clear that he was barely tolerating fellows like me, as he said I taught Christians it was "okay" for them to kill for their government when it "commands" them to do so. I assure you that I do not believe, nor have I ever taught, anything of the sort. I do not think the responsibilities of citizenship are so easily discerned, as my accuser suggests. Furthermore, I do not believe one's citizenship obligations should ever interfere with the Christian's duty to *obey God rather than men.*[26] Thus, I believe there are times when a Christian must refuse to serve his country, and that if he didn't, he would certainly be involving himself in sin. In other words, the state does not possess ultimate authority. Instead, it

---

[25] See I Pet. 2:14; Tit. 3:1; Rom. 13:1-7.
[26] See Acts 5:29.

possesses only delegated authority,[27] and any government that doesn't recognize this is idolatrous.

True Patriotism Is Limited Patriotism

Consequently, whatever patriotism is, it cannot—indeed, it must not—automatically exempt itself from the charge that *"in his own eyes he flatters himself too much to detect or hate his sin."*[28] Whatever it is, patriotism should not imprudently suppose that, by invoking the name of God in slogans, it will tether the Almighty to its cause any more successfully than rebellious Israel did when Eli's sons took the ark of the covenant out of mothballs and propped it like a talisman before the armies marching against the Philistines.[29] True patriotism does not permit itself to be manipulated by media mantras into a pumped-up frenzy that drowns out all other voices—particularly the voice of Jesus, who said, "Render to Caesar what is Caesar's and to God what is God's." To the state, then, and when such is just, obedient servants present their bodies and wills for the national defense; to God, a "contrite and humble spirit."[30] As a result, there need be no contradiction, no conflict of interest. So, like Daniel, who knew how to "seek the peace of the city" to which God had carried him into exile,[31] but who, along with Hananiah, Mishael and Azariah, would not bow to its "image of gold,"[32] the New Testament Christian needs to reflect the godly patriotism the Lord enjoins for His priesthood of spiritual pilgrims who, in every age, sojourn in Babylon while "longing for a better country."[33] "Pray," He says, "to the Lord for [your country]; for in its peace you will have peace."[34]

---

[27] See Jn. 19:11.
[28] Psa. 36:2, NIV.
[29] See I Sam. 4.
[30] Isa. 57:15.
[31] See Jer. 29:7a.
[32] Dan. 3.
[33] Heb. 11:16, NIV.
[34] Jer. 29:7b.

I, for one, do not believe the only choice of action for the thinking Christian is to be found in the tweedledee of mindless, hysterical hawkishness, or the tweedledum of half-baked, limpish pacifism. Instead, there ought to be a loyalty to one's country based on truth, not lies, and a manly, unflinching patriotism that is based on reality and not popular fiction. The causes of Justice and Righteousness today, like always, call for leaders and soldiers who are prudent, courageous, self-controlled and just. These need to possess the virtues that will enable them to know not just *why* and *when* to go to war, but *how* to properly fight it, and finally, *when to stop it*. We need defenders distinguished by the kind of character that empowers them to pursue every honorable avenue for victory against the enemy, but who are, in the end, resolved to suffer death before dishonor. Where better to find this character and these virtues than in the Christian?

The Christian Soldier

The Christian fights for justice because God is like this, in that He uses force to check evil and bring justice. So, the Christian uses force to restrain evil because this is what God is like, and because God is like this, the Christian does not sin (i.e., he is acting godly) when he uses legitimate force, and this remains true even when this force is deadly force. Furthermore, as God's use of force is a product of His love for His creatures, and as it is clear that God even loves those whom He kills, the Christian, just like God, must love his enemies even when called upon to righteously take their lives. Any acts that are not God-like are morally suspect for the Christian soldier. The acts of a soldier can never be one of personal vengeance.[35] Therefore, a just war is something Christians participate in out of loving obedience to God and in conformity to His ways. In his personal relationships, the Christian acts in love toward others as God has always required His followers to do. But when he chooses to participate in government as a soldier or law

---

[35] See Matt. 5:38-41.

enforcement officer, the Christian acts in accord with the God-ordained mandate given to the state. There is no contradiction here, as the Christian is free to participate in any legitimate function of government, even war, without violating the restrictions God places on him in his personal affairs.

On the other hand, those who think the Christian, simply by virtue of his Christianity, gets to opt out of doing justice are sorely mistaken. They fail, in their elitism, to comprehend what being a faithful subject of God is all about.[36] As such, they delegate the "dirty hands" duty of doing justice to unredeemed sinners. In doing so, they fail to fully understand the nature of God (a nature that demands justice) and denigrate the very character of those people God has appointed over the administration of justice—people the apostle Paul called "God's ministers to you for good."[37] How unfortunate it is that many of God's people, past and present, because they have failed to rightly divide God's word,[38] have majored in the theology of calling good evil and evil good.[39]

Can a Christian participate in war? Yes, when the doing of justice demands it. Can a Christian participate in just any war? No, he most certainly cannot. If the war is not morally justified, and by this I mean consistent with the precepts and principles taught in the Bible, a Christian would not remain "unspotted" by participating in it. What's more, a Christian could not participate even in a just war if the *means* being used to fight it are unjust. Consequently, the Christian must always sit in judgment upon the activities of his government, supporting it when it is right, but refusing to do so when it is wrong. This, I believe, is part of being what a true Christian is all about.

---

[36] See Mic. 8:8 and Matt. 23:23.
[37] Rom. 13:4.
[38] See 2 Tim. 2:15.
[39] See Isa. 5:20.

Serving In The Military

Does this mean I heartily recommend military service? No, it does not. Serving in the military is dangerous business, and I'm not just referring to the obvious physical dangers of the job. More important than the physical dangers are the moral and spiritual dangers confronting the warrior. Soldiering isn't easy, particularly for the enlisted man. By an act of Congress, commissioned officers are declared not just officers, but "gentlemen" as well. Therefore, a higher moral code has traditionally been forced upon officers rather than on the regular enlisted personnel. This means that cursing, gambling, whoremongering, and other such vices are less likely to be eschewed among the enlisted ranks than among the officers. In fact, it is fair to say that such crassness has always been commonplace within the lower ranks of the military—and I'm talking about any military here. I wish it were not so, but it is. Consequently, the man who enlists in the military will have more opportunities to stray from the straight and narrow than his civilian cohort. Indeed, much peer pressure will be brought to bear on the Christian who refuses to go along. As a result, he will be branded a "mama's boy," a "girly boy," or even a "queer."

Additionally, the Christian will at times—and sometimes for long periods of time—be unable to assemble with those of like precious faith. Deprived of the fellowship of fellow saints, the Christian soldier will be left with his spiritual flanks dangerously exposed. If, for any reason, he's failed to put on the whole armor of God,[40] then he will, no doubt, be wounded, perhaps seriously or even fatally. Not many Christians could honorably serve in the military without compromising at least some of their convictions. Now, I'm not saying it can't be done, mind you; only that it would be extremely difficult for the average Christian. But after all, the true warrior, whether enlisted man or officer, is anything but average. The fictional model for such a person is the knight of the Middle Ages, and in Malory's *The Death of Arthur*, the knight

---

[40] See Eph. 6:10-17.

Lancelot is pictured as "the meekest man and the gentlest that ever ate in the hall among ladies" and also as "the sternest knight...that ever put spear in the rest."[41]

Of course, the Christian will understand that this chivalric ideal of the godly warrior (consisting of a combination of gentleness and meekness mixed, when necessary, with great violence) was provided by the likes of Joshua and David *et al.*—warriors spawned by the God who is Himself a "Man of War" or "Warrior."[42] Christianity, like the Judaism before it, is not for wimps. Whether involved in carnal or spiritual warfare, God's warriors are called upon to "Be on the alert, stand firm in the faith, act like men, be strong."[43] This kind of expected behavior places one under a "double demand," as C.S. Lewis referred to it, for knightly Sir Lancelot represented not an ideal mean between meekness and violence, but the highest degree of both at the same time. When striving faithfully to serve God and country, this is exactly what Christian soldiers do. They know that the greatest evil in war is not death, nor is it even killing. Instead, the greatest evil is killing unjustly. Consequently, just wars require just people to wage them. The virtues of wisdom, justice, courage, and self-control must guide the Christian in his decision as to when he can make his country's war his war. To "serve and protect" the innocent is the primary motive for the Christian's decision to participate in war. In doing so, he must realize that the chivalrous character, which requires one to be fierce to the nth degree and meek to the nth degree, must always be emulated. However, such fierceness and meekness do not grow together naturally, and to acquire such a character is no easy matter. Only in the Christian do we find the best chance for this kind of character, for it is, after all is said and done, the kind of character exhibited by our Lord and Savior Jesus Christ. Consequently, the chivalrous character is *not* a work of nature, but a work of art. This means that if this kind of character is not espoused by the church and cultivated by the military, it will likely

---

[41] XXL.13.
[42] See various translations of Ex. 15:3.
[43] I Cor. 16:13, NASB.

not be acquired at all. And therefore, after all is said and done, if there are no chivalrous soldiers, then no war—however just its cause—will be fought justly.

May God richly bless all chivalrous soldiers as they seek to faithfully fulfill both aspects of this "double demand," exhibiting at the same time a fierceness and meekness best found in those who have, by means of God's magnificent grace, cultivated the wisdom of serpents and the harmlessness of doves.[44]

In the next chapter, we'll look at the service of one such soldier.

---

[44] See Matt. 10:16.

Chapter 4

An Example Of Salty Chivalry

Johnny Micheal (that's the way it's spelled) "Mike" Spann, a United States Marine and paramilitary officer in the CIA's Directorate of Operations, Special Activities Division, was the first American to die in combat in Afghanistan. He was shot and killed on November 25, 2001, in a prison uprising by captured Taliban and al-Qaeda operatives at the Kala Jangi fortress in the Northern Afghan city of Mazar-e Sharif. He was from the small town of Winfield, Alabama, about halfway between Birmingham and Tupelo, Mississippi. He was a Criminal Justice graduate from Auburn University. He was also a New Testament Christian.

At his funeral at Arlington National Cemetery, where he received full military honors, his wife, Shannon, in her final goodbye to his flag-draped coffin, said *"Simper Fi, my love." Simper fi*, which is short for *simper fidelis*, is the Marine Corps' motto and means "always faithful." Whether he was in all things faithful is a decision best left to the One who knows all things perfectly and is, therefore, incapable of making an error in judgment. But, it bodes well for Mike Spann that the wife to whom he had sworn his love believed him to be *simper fi*, and that the grateful country he served thought him to be faithful to the last ounce of devotion. These serve as beacons of hope that this Christian soldier faithfully fulfilled his "whole duty" to the Lord God Almighty, the Ruler of all that is. At Spann's burial service, the preacher tellingly said:

> Mike Spann was the kind of man we dream of growing up to be when we are boys—tough, kind, strong, fair, fully committed to God, to family, to country. He was a warrior in the highest, best sense of that word. So like David—[he was] courageous and

prepared because his highest aim was to please God, protect his family, and preserve his nation.

George J. Tenet, the Director of Central Intelligence, said in his remarks:

> Here today, in American soil, we lay to lasting rest an American hero. United in loss and in sorrow, we are united, as well, in our reverence for the timeless virtues upon which Mike Spann shaped his life—virtues for which he ultimately gave his life.
>
> Dignity. Decency. Bravery. Liberty.
>
> From his earliest days, Mike not only knew what was right, he worked to do what was right. At home and school in Alabama. As a United States Marine. As an officer of the Central Intelligence Agency. And as the head of his own, young family.
>
> And it was in the quest for right that Mike at his country's call went to Afghanistan. To that place of danger and terror, he sought to bring justice and freedom. And to our nation—which he held so close to his heart—he sought to bring a still greater measure of strength and security.
>
> For Mike understood that it is not enough simply to dream of a better, safer world. He understood that it has to be built—with passion and dedication, in the face of obstacles, in the face of evil.
>
> Those who took him from us will be neither deeply mourned nor long remembered. But Mike Spann will be forever part of the treasured legacy of free peoples everywhere—as we each owe him an immense, unpayable debt of honor and gratitude.
>
> His example is our inspiration. His sacrifice is our strength.
>
> For the men and women of the Central Intelligence Agency, he remains the rigorous and resolute colleague. The professional who took great pride in his difficult and demanding work. The patriot who knew that information saves lives, and that its collection is a risk worth taking.

May God bless Mike Spann—an American of courage— and may God bless those who love and miss him, and all who carry on the noble work that he began.[1]

I think these are fitting tributes to a fallen warrior, but thinking about Mike Spann and those like him, I feel compelled to ask the questions listed in the subtitle below.

But Who Are These People, And From Whence Do They Come?

In *The Letter to Diognetus*, which is believed to have been written in A.D. 130, an individual by the name of Mathetes undertook to explain to a pagan reader the way it is with these strange people called Christians. He said, in part:

> For the Christians are distinguished from other men neither by country, nor language, nor the customs which they observe. For they neither inhabit cities of their own, nor employ a peculiar form of speech, nor lead a life which is marked out by any singularity. The course of conduct which they follow has not been devised by any speculation or deliberation of inquisitive men; nor do they, like some, proclaim themselves the advocates of any merely human doctrines. But, inhabiting Greek as well as barbarian cities, according as the lot of each of them has determined, and following the customs of the natives in respect to clothing, food, and the rest of their ordinary conduct, they display to us their wonderful and confessedly striking method of life. They dwell in their own countries, but simply as sojourners. As citizens, they share in all things with others, and yet endure all things as if foreigners. Every foreign land is to them as their native country, and every land of their birth as a land of strangers. They marry, as do all [others]; they beget children; but they do not destroy their offspring. They have a common table, but not a

---

[1] George J. Tenet, Funeral of Johnny Micheal Spann, Arlington National Cementary, December 10, 2001.

common bed. They are in the flesh, but they do not live after the flesh. They pass their days on earth, but they are citizens of heaven. They obey the prescribed laws, and at the same time surpass the laws by their lives. They love all men, and are persecuted by all. They are unknown and condemned; they are put to death, and re-stored to life. They are poor, yet make many rich; they are in lack of all things, and yet abound in all; they are dishonoured, and yet in their very dishonour are glorified. They are evil spoken of, and yet are justified; they are reviled, and bless; they are insulted, and repay the insult with honour; they do good, yet are punished as evil-doers. When punished, they rejoice as if quickened into life; they are as-sailed by the Jews as foreigners, and are persecuted by the Greeks; yet those who hate them are unable to assign any reason for their hatred.

To sum up all in one word—what the soul is in the body, that Christians are in the world. The soul is dispersed through all the members of the body, and Christians are scattered through all the cities of the world. The soul dwells in the body, yet is not of the body; and Christians dwell in the world, yet are not of the world.

For almost two millennia, these "alien citizens," still far from their New Jerusalem home, have followed a course of action they believe prescribed in the Bible—a course that compels fidelity to the well-being of their homeland *in time* before the *end of time.* The so-called "Just War" doctrine has emerged as one product of this attempted fidelity. The doctrine, articulated by the many different classes of men who have claimed to be Christian, teaches that just war, although occasioned by evil, is not, in and of itself, evil; nor is it, as is commonly held today, even a necessary evil. On the contrary, if just, war is a positive duty, the doing of which, even though it frequently involves much suffering, is to be counted as a good. However, the pacifist who has been unconvinced by the non-pacifist arguments made in this study will ask, "But what would Jesus do?" or "Can you imagine Jesus flying a stealth bomber or involved in a commando raid?" As a December, 2001 editorial in *First Things* points out:

One might as well ask if you can imagine Jesus driving a bus, editing a magazine, or being a tenured professor in a religious studies department. The question is not what Jesus would do but what he would have us do.[2]

This, I think, is an excellent point. Of course, the pacifist will answer this question one way while others, like me, will answer that in obedience to the command to love one's neighbor, the Christian is duty-bound to defend the innocent by engaging in a just war against a murderous aggressor. Although genuine pacifists—and I'm not talking about those who are just plain cowards and don't want to fight—may be intensely sincere, they are nevertheless monumentally wrong. Although the personal ethic that has us giving way to violence-prone people is not only scriptural, but wise,[3] nonviolent resistance to the aggression American citizens are now facing is a tactic that is utterly implausible and, I believe, completely unscriptural. First, the naive belief that aggression can be effectively resisted if we'll only be nice and understanding to terrorists is not just idealistic, but it is just plain dumb! Second, civil government was ordained by God to take life, if necessary, in order to protect its citizens and punish evildoers, and all this consistent with the principles of Justice and Righteousness taught in the Bible.[4] Consequently, it is time for pacifists to get themselves "up to speed" on this extremely important subject. When they do so, they'll quit looking down their spiritual noses at those who understand that fidelity to God's word demands the unpleasant as well as the pleasant. The God of the Bible, the One who expects His followers to be 24-hours-a-day disciples, never taught that the living they do for Him is to be compartmentalized into that which is secular and that which is sa-

---

[2] Refer to http://www.firstthings.com/.
[3] See Matt. 5:39.
[4] See Rom. 13:1-7, 1 Pet. 2:13-14.

cred. Either Jesus Christ is Lord of all, or He's Lord of nothing. Please, Lord, give us more of these salty, chivalrous Christians.[5]

In the next chapter, we'll deal with what I think is a key to understanding this difficult subject.

---

[5] See Matt. 5:13.

Chapter 5

But What About The Sermon On The Mount?

There are no more widely known sayings of Jesus than the ones recorded in Matthew 5:1-7:29, commonly referred to as the Sermon on the Mount. How one interprets these teachings plays a big part in how he views the question of war. If one sees Jesus' moral and ethical teachings here as a new and unique set of ethics, then it is very likely he will lean more toward the pacifist position. On the other hand, if one believes the ethics articulated in this sermon to be a declaration of the deeper meanings of the "law and the prophets" (a Hebrew idiom denoting the entire Old Testament), then he is more likely to take a non-pacifist position.

Pacifists, along with a great number of Christians, generally believe the Lord's teaching in the Sermon on the Mount *supersedes* the precepts and principles set forth in the Old Testament. They believe Jesus' purpose in this sermon was to annul the ethical code of the Mosaical covenant by announcing a new and loftier morality. But it is just here that many pacifists part company with their fellow Christians, for radical pacifists reject the idea that the Sermon on the Mount pertains fundamentally to personal ethics and insist the commandments set forth by Jesus here are to be inflexibly adhered to in *every relationship* of life. Consequently, their view calls for a radical withdrawal from government and society.

Although it's not possible to speak of an "official position" of the Restoration Movement in this country, it is a documented fact that the pacifist sentiments mentioned above were reflected in many of its most influential preachers, writers, and editors. It was just such a view, no doubt, that motivated the pacifism of Alexander Campbell, Tolbert Fanning, Benjamin Franklin, Moses Lard,

Robert Milligan, J. W. McGarvey, David Lipscomb *et al.* And it is just such a view that continues to be reflected in the lives of more than a few New Testament Christians. I am of the opinion that such an interpretation of the Sermon on the Mount was a mistake *then*, and it's a mistake *now*.

On the other hand, many non-pacifists believe there is essential agreement between Jesus and the Old Testament in ethical matters; that the ethics of Jesus' teachings are not a radical departure from the law and the prophets; that the moral requirements of the two covenants are not fundamentally different. Consequently, the purpose of the Sermon on the Mount was not to revise or reverse Mosaic ethics, but to reaffirm their fuller and necessary implications. Of course, it's important to understand that the Sermon on the Mount does not exhaust all the Christian's social and personal responsibilities. When a Christian fails to realize this, he is vulnerable to several erroneous positions, one of which is pacifism.

The argument that Jesus was replacing the moral standard of the Old Testament with a new and improved version stands in direct contradiction of what He himself clearly announced, for in Matthew 5:17 Jesus made it clear He was not abolishing the law and the prophets. The Greek word here for "abolish" is *katalusai*, and it means "to dissolve or abrogate." So, to say that Jesus did, in fact, abrogate the morality of the Old Testament is to place Him in a position of contradicting His own words, which is unacceptable for the Bible believer. Further, in this same passage Jesus announced His intention was to *fulfill* the law and the prophets. The word "fulfill," from the Greek *pleroo*, means variously "to accomplish or obey, to bring out the full meaning, to complete, or abundantly supply," and it is clear that Jesus did all these by His own obedience to the Law,[1] by satisfying its demands for justice,[2] by being the One to whom it pointed,[3] and by fully explaining it, or fleshing it out, as He did here in this sermon. In fact, it should be

---

[1] See Heb. 10:7-9.
[2] See Gal. 3:10-14.
[3] See Matt. 1:22, 2:15, Jn. 5:39, Gal. 3:24.

apparent that those who heard Him speak that day would have been more likely to understand Him in this latter sense. Besides, it should be clear why Jesus would have felt compelled to declare His motives up front, for what He would subsequently teach in this sermon would glaringly contradict the morality being taught by the scribes and Pharisees. And as it was these scribes and Pharisees who the people commonly thought to be the true inter-preters of the Law, it was necessary for Him to make it clear that He was not, in any way, contradicting the Law of Moses, only the traditional misinterpretations of the scribes and Pharisees.

Because one's interpretation of the Sermon on the Mount is so important to understanding the war question, I believe I must do more than just make the claim my argument is correct. Instead, I must give convincing proof. This will involve the exegeses of a seg-ment of the Lord's Sermon on the Mount, along with another sec-tion of Scripture where the Lord defends His disciples from a charge that claimed they had profaned the Sabbath. This will take considerable space and time, but I believe you may find the jour-ney worth the effort.

A Look At Matthew 12:1-8

Before getting to the series of controversial contrasts Jesus makes in Matthew 5:21-48, it is important to grasp the full impact of Jesus' Sermon on the Mount, for it is from this sermon forward that we see the scribes' and Pharisees' hatred for Jesus growing to the point when it culminates in their murdering Him with the help of a corrupt Roman official. In other words, when the Lord put these scribes and Pharisees on notice with His Sermon on the Mount, it was clear to them that He was a threat to their influence and power. Consequently, they would stop at nothing to destroy Him.[4] So, let's look at Matthew 12:1-8 and make some observa-tions about it:

---

[4] See Matt. 12:14; 26:3-4.

At that time Jesus went through the grainfields on the Sabbath. And His disciples were hungry, and began to pluck heads of grain and to eat. And when the Pharisees saw it, they said to Him, "Look, Your disciples are doing what is not lawful to do on the Sabbath!" But He said to them, "Have you not read what David did when he was hungry, he and those who were with him: how he entered the house of God and ate the showbread which was not lawful for him to eat, nor for those who were with him, but only for the priests? Or have you not read in the law that on the Sabbath the priests in the temple profane the Sabbath, and are blameless? Yet I say to you that in this place there is One greater than the temple. But if you had known what this means, 'I desire mercy and not sacrifice,' you would not have condemned the guiltless. For the Son of Man is Lord even of the Sabbath.

The Pharisees had always been a minority group, but during Jesus' time they were the religious power in Palestine. Initially, they were known as the *Chasidim* (pious ones), a group that arose during the 2nd century B.C. to protect and preserve the Jews' religious heritage from the influence of Greek culture. In their zealousness for things Jewish, they espoused radical doctrinal views—views that were later reflected in the Pharisees. Especially influential was the Chasidim's penchant for what would become the rabbinical view of oral tradition: the belief that Moses also instituted oral law as a part of the Jew's religion, with this law being made up of the traditional interpretations of the rabbis. In this regard, it is interesting to note the Mishnah, a 2nd-century A.D. compilation of earlier rabbinical views, as it reflects the extremes to which the Sabbath labor law was viewed by the rabbis:

[He is culpable] that takes out rope enough to make a handle for a basket...

[He is culpable] that takes out leather enough to make an amulet, or vellum enough to write on it the shortest passage in the phylacteries, namely, *Hear, O Israel*...; or ink enough to write two letters, or eye-paint enough to paint one eye.

If a man took out a loaf into the public domain he is culpable; if two men took it out they are not culpable.

If a man removed his fingernails by means of his nails or his teeth, and so, too, if [he pulled out] the hair of his head, or his mustache or his beard; and so, too, if a woman dressed her hair or painted her eyelids or reddened [her face] - such a one R. Eliezer declares liable [to a sin-offering]; but the Sages forbid [acts the like of these only] by virtue of the [rabbinically ordained] Sabbath rest.

He is culpable that writes two letters, whether with his right hand or with his left, whether the same or different letters, whether in different inks or in any language.

A man may fold up his garments [that he wears on the Sabbath] as many as four or five times. Beds may be spread on the night of Sabbath for the Sabbath day, but not on the Sabbath for the night following the Sabbath.

A man may not shift about the straw on the bed with his hand but he may shift it about with his body.

If a man's hand or foot is dislocated he may not pour cold water over it, but he may wash it after his usual fashion.

It was just such extremism that caused the frequent confrontations between Jesus and the Pharisees. The ruler of a synagogue, displeased with Jesus' healing of an infirmed woman on the Sabbath, protested, "There are six days on which men ought to work; therefore come and be healed on them, and not on the Sabbath."[5] After the Lord healed a lame man, the Jews said, "It is the Sabbath; it is not lawful for you to carry your bed."[6] In this account, it says the "Jews sought all the more to kill Him."[7] Therefore, when Jesus' disciples plucked and ate grain on the Sabbath, the Pharisees were bent on blood when they said, "Look, Your disciples are doing what is not lawful to do on the Sabbath!"[8] But Luke 6:2, which says, "Why are You doing what is not lawful to do on the Sabbath?," makes it clear their ire was directed more at Jesus than His disciples (i.e., they were attacking the Lord's disciples in

---

[5] Lk. 13:14.
[6] Jn. 5:10.
[7] Jn. 5:18.
[8] Matt. 12:2.

order to get at Him). However, it was not God's Law, but their man-made traditions, that formed the basis of their charge. According to Jesus, it was not unlawful for His disciples to be "plucking" heads of grain and "rubbing them in their hands" on the Sabbath, as the account recorded in Luke 6:1 says.

Nevertheless, the Pharisees were convinced the rules of rabbinic oral tradition, rules which were alleged to be inferences and applications of the law itself, made it absolutely clear that they believed Jesus and His disciples were guilty of profaning the Sabbath, for in the *Patres Traditionum,* it said:

> He who reaps on the Sabbath is chargeable; and to pluck ears is a species of reaping. And whoever breaks off anything from its stalk is chargeable under the specification of reaping. The deeds which make a man chargeable with stoning and death if he does them presumptuously, or with a sacrifice if he sins ignorantly, are either generic or derivative. Thirty-nine kinds of the generic are enumerated: to plow, to sow, to reap, to bind sheaves, to thresh, to winnow, to grind, to pound, to powder, etc., to shear sheep, to dye wool, etc.; and the derivatives are of the same class and likeness: furrowing = plowing; cutting up vegetables = grinding; plucking ears = reaping.[9]

In contrast, Jesus made it clear that He and His disciples were not guilty of profaning the Sabbath, and that it was actually the Pharisees' understanding of the Law that was in error.[10] Deuteronomy 23:25 says, "When you come into your neighbor's standing grain, you may pluck the heads with your hand, but you shall not use a sickle on your neighbor's standing grain." Although this passage does not specifically address the Sabbath law, it is interesting to observe the difference the Scriptures make between *plucking* and *sickling.* Plucking your neighbor's grain would not be considered stealing, while using a sickle would. Why? Because it seems clear when one "works" on (i.e., uses a sickle) or

---

[9] In R.C.H. Lenski, *Commentary of the New Testament, Matthew,* page 461.
[10] See Matt. 12:7.

"harvests" his neighbors grain, he's making or exerting an effort to take what does not belong to him (i.e., he's stealing his neighbor's grain). But when he simply plucks the grain with his hand, he is only doing so to satisfy hunger, which puts him in the category of eating, not working. When one extends this principle to the work prohibitions of the Sabbath law, which were never designed to interfere with a man eating or taking nourishment, then a reasonable person would conclude that Jesus' disciples were not violating the Law of Moses when walking through grain fields on the Sabbath, plucking and eating the grain. That this is a right conclusion is verified by Jesus—who was, after all, the "Lord of the Sabbath" (verse 8)—when He pronounced His disciples "guiltless" (verse 7). *(Incidentally, being Lord of the Sabbath did not mean, as some have concluded, that Jesus was free to arbitrarily violate or change the Sabbath law as it suited Him. What it means is that if anyone was in a position to fully understand the Sabbath it was He. Jesus was the One who instituted the Sabbath and, as Lord of it, He knew what it involved, when it was being profaned, and when it was being misstated by the likes of these Pharisees.)*

There is another argument Jesus made in regard to this that is not recorded in Matthew 12:1-8 and it is very important to understanding this issue. Referring to the same episode, Mark 2:27 has the Lord saying, "The Sabbath was made for man, and not man for the Sabbath." By the steady stream of minute and often absurd requirements articulated in their oral tradition, the Pharisees had reversed the order Jesus here mentions. God had created the Sabbath for man, in that it provided him not just the time to rest physically, but the time also to attend to his spiritual needs. The Jews had turned this order topsy-turvy. Instead of the Sabbath being created for man, and therefore a blessing, they had come to reflect the idea that man had been created in order to keep the Sabbath, viewing it then as a heavy and vexing burden to be borne no matter how man fared. The Sabbath, according to these Jews, had to be kept regardless of man's circumstances. Therefore, although Jesus' disciples were hungry and only doing that which the Law permitted (viz., eating, not harvesting), they were falsely accused of "doing what is not lawful to do on the Sabbath" (Matthew 12:2b). "But," Jesus said in His response to these self-righteous hypocrites in Matthew 12:7, "if you had known what this means, 'I desire mercy and not sacrifice,' you would not have condemned the guiltless." Jesus had already referred to Hosea 6:6 in Matthew 9:13. There He said, "Go and learn what this means: 'I desire mercy and not sacrifice.'" It is especially interesting that the Lord bade these folks to "Go and learn," a Rabinnic model that demanded of the hearers further contemplation and insight. So, the Lord has now delivered a double rebuke to these Pharisees, treating them first as learners rather than teachers, and second as beginners who were so ignorant of the Scriptures they were unable to properly interpret them. If the Sabbath was made for man, and Jesus said it was, then the *requirements* (i.e., the needs) of man will always qualify those things enjoined by the Sabbath. Because the Pharisees didn't understand this, they were engaged in condemning the guiltless.

Of course, the fences these Pharisees had built around the Law in order to not transgress it were not, in and of themselves, wrong. In fact, gospel preachers do this when they teach Christians not to get so close to sin before stopping, lest they sometimes find themselves falling over the precipice. In other words, prudence is a virtue worth cultivating—a fence worth erecting, if you will. However, when our fences are transformed into the Law itself, then we, like the Pharisees of old, will find ourselves in the position of condemning the guiltless. This, I think, is exactly what some pacifists are willing to do to their brethren who espouse the position I've defended in this study. As one of these wrote:

> To be candid, I would feel uncomfortable worshipping in church where my opponent's doctrine [a non-pacifist position] was taught from the pulpit. I would also feel uncomfortable financially supporting any evangelist or employing him in a corporate work of a local congregation (such as a gospel meeting) if he continued to teach error on the "civil government" issue.[11]

---

[11] I have chosen not to give the citation in order to protect, in this case, the guilty.

In his commentary on the book of Matthew, Kenneth Chumbley warns:

> In each generation there are different groups that fit the category of publicans and sinners; and there are religionists who are long on sacrifice but short on mercy, who are more interested in upholding their sectarianism than in helping the hurting, and who are critical of any who ignore their rules. And such Pharisaism is as abhorrent now as when Jesus encountered it.[12]

These words are well worth remembering, for the non-pacifist as well as the pacifist. We cannot, indeed we must not, make our conscience another man's guide. When we do so, we become modern-day Pharisees.

Because the aforementioned brother (not Chumbley, but the unnamed debater) is willing to inflict his misinterpretation and misapplication of the Scriptures on those of us who disagree with him, he is willing to withdraw fellowship, treating us as unrepentant sinners. In doing so, he demonstrates himself an élitist (i.e., Pharisee) of the first order. As such, he not only "condemns the guiltless," but he shows his ignorance of the "weightier matters of the Law"[13]—justice, mercy and faith. *Justice* demands we aid the victims of injustice; *mercy* requires us to demonstrate compassion on those who are being unjustly treated; and faith, after all is said and done, demands the doing of both justice and mercy. Therefore, to walk by faith in this present world (i.e., doing justice and loving mercy) is not withdrawing into asceticism, divorcing oneself from the *people* and *events* of *time* and *space*; it is, instead, being salt and light to a lost and dying world.[14] This brings us now to an examination of Jesus' Sermon on the Mount, a sermon that teaches what it really means to be a child of God.

---

[12] Kenneth L. Chumbley, *The Gospel of Matthew*, page 175.
[13] Matt. 23:23.
[14] See Matt. 5:13-17.

A Closer Examination Of The Contrasts Jesus Made

The series of contrasts in Matthew 5:21-48 have caused many to believe that Jesus was pitting Himself against "the law and the prophets." However, the most reasonable conclusion is that the Lord was refuting the rabbinical perversions and false interpretations the Jewish people had commonly come to accept. Such a conflict was inevitable, for Jesus came into this world not to make men religious (the Jews already had plenty of this), but to make them religiously right. In this regard, He did not come to bring peace, but a sword.[15] Consequently, the scene for Jesus' confrontation with the Jewish leaders (viz., the scribes, Sadducees and Pharisees) was set when His forerunner, John the Baptist, challenged the Sadducees and Pharisees with: "Brood of vipers! Who has warned you to flee from the wrath to come?"[16] But Jesus' actual confrontation with the Pharisees begins with the Sermon on the Mount. It continues to intensify throughout the rest of His earthly ministry, ultimately culminating with His death on the cross. It starts with the Lord saying, "For I say to you, that unless your righteousness exceeds the righteousness of the scribes and Pharisees, you will by no means enter the kingdom of heaven"[17] and ends with His Temple address where He made His "Woe to you..." and "Fools and blind!" charges.[18] But even before this scathing rebuke, the Pharisees had made up their minds to destroy Jesus.[19] The reason being that in His conflict with them over their Sabbath law interpretations and applications,[20] He had not only called into question their understanding of the Law, but their entire theological system. Realizing His continued popularity would threaten their continued leadership, they were now bent on destroying Him.

---

[15] See Matt. 10:34.
[16] Matt. 3:7b.
[17] Matt. 5:20.
[18] See Matt. 23:2-36.
[19] See Matt. 12:14.
[20] See Matt. 12:1-14.

As has already been pointed out, Jesus, in Matthew 5:21-48, was not attacking the Law, which He clearly said He had not come to destroy,[21] but the oral tradition which had originally been created as a hedge of protection around the Law and had now risen to the status of the Law itself. This means that what Jesus said in the Sermon on the Mount was not to be viewed as a new set of ethical norms, as pacifist brethren think, but as the Lord's explication of the ethical requirements of the Law unperverted by rabbinical think-sos. For proof of this, let's examine the verses themselves.

Matthew 5:21 "You have heard that it was said to those of old, 'You shall not murder, and whoever murders will be in danger of the judgment.'"

Six times in verses 21-48 (viz., 21, 27, 31, 33, 38, 43) Jesus says, "You have heard it said." With each of these "You have heard" statements, the contrast Jesus is making is between the true teachings of Moses' Law and the false teachings of rabbinic tradition. Here the Lord refers to rabbinic teaching about the sixth commandment, which condemned murder.

Matthew 5:22 "But I say to you that whoever is angry with his brother without a cause shall be in danger of the judgment. And whoever says to his brother, 'Raca!' shall be in danger of the council. But whoever says, 'You fool!' shall be in danger of hell fire."

When Jesus says, "But I say unto you," He was speaking as the Word, the Divine Logos, the Supreme Lawgiver. He had started using it back in verse 18. The prophets had tended to say "Thus saith the Lord," and His apostles would later say "It is written," but Jesus' use of "I say unto you," shouts His divine authority, for such language would appear totally unacceptable coming from the lips of a mere man. Who better to explain the Law than the Divine Lawgiver Himself?

The problem with what the scribes and Pharisees had said about murder—i.e., "Thou shall not murder, and whoever murders will be in danger of the judgment"—was that they had not

---

[21] See verse 17.

gone far enough. What the rabbinic tradition expounded was the law itself, and that murderers needed to be subject to the courts. Not a word about what this commandment required of men's hearts. So what these Jews now hear Jesus saying is quite different than what they had heard the scribes and Pharisees declare. Again, the Lord's conflict is not with Moses and what he said; the conflict is with the rabbinic tradition that so grossly ignored the implications of the sixth commandment—i.e., that God, in giving the sixth commandment, never had in view only a civil law and civil court, but addressed the hearts of those who would be His children—hearts which must not be filled with unjust anger and ugly epithets. 1 John 3:15 perfectly demonstrates what Jesus had in mind here: "Whoever hates his brother is a murderer, and you know that no murderer has eternal life abiding in him." So, God declares the unjust anger that accompanies murder, along with the ugly epithets that go with it, as equally offensive as murder itself.

However, it would be a serious mistake to think Jesus is condemning any and all anger. He's not. "Without a cause" makes it clear He is not referring to *every* instance of anger.[22] Righteous indignation is a legitimate response to ungodliness,[23] and even God Himself is angry with the wicked every day.[24] In fact, there were times when even the meek and lowly Jesus demonstrated anger.[25] A man or woman who can't get angry is a person who will fail to do justice and love mercy.[26] Anger is the emotional power behind civil justice, and those Christians who didn't feel anger toward those who caused those airplanes to be flown into the World Trade Center on September 11, 2001 were not acting like God's children. And as it relates to this study, let me say that I believe pacifists who, in the name of Christ, refuse to pursue justice in the present war on terrorism, do Christ, and the religion that bears His name,

---

[22] See Eph. 4:26.
[23] See Rom. 12:9.
[24] See Psa. 7:11.
[25] See Mk. 3:5, John 2:17.
[26] See Mic. 6:8.

a disservice. Like the Pharisees of old, they are zealous for the law of Christ, but pervert it with their misinterpretation and misapplications, making the doing of justice a "dirty-hands" affair.

At the same time, and because anger is an extremely volatile emotion that can be easily tainted by our sin-sick natures, we must strive to keep all anger in check (again, see Ephesians 4:26). Civil government does not condemn a man for having murderous thoughts, but God certainly does. If the Jews of Jesus' day had understood this they would not have been acting like they were. And if New Testament Christians understood this today, they would not be biting and devouring each other as they sometimes do. With this in mind, I want to quote once again from Chumbley's *The Gospel of Matthew*:

> Though some see here progressive stages of crime (murder, Raca, fool) and punishment (judgment, council, hell fire), it seems better to regard these terms as parallel references. Christ isn't saying there is never a situation in which a man deserves to be called a fool (7.26-27, 23.17, Gal. 3.1) or that calling a man a fool is worse than calling him Raca, which is worse than being angry at him without a cause. Instead, He is teaching that insulting language—name calling, racial, ethnic, and social slurs, etc.—that demeans a fellow human being is condemned by God. (It is also worth noting that an ungodly attitude toward another can manifest itself in silence, as well as in speech. "Silence is the most perfect expression of scorn" [G.B. Shaw] and giving another the "silent treatment" or a "cold shoulder" can be as ungodly as the use of insulting, derogatory language.)

Matthew 5:23-26 "Therefore if you bring your gift to the altar, and there remember that your brother has something against you, leave your gift there before the altar, and go your way. First be reconciled to your brother, and then come and offer your gift. Agree with your adversary quickly, while you are on the way with him, lest your adversary deliver you to the judge, the judge hand you over to the officer, and you be thrown into prison. Assuredly, I say to you, you will by no means get out of there till you have paid the last penny."

"Therefore" begins the practical application of what the Lord has said in verse 22. Anger (ours and the other person's) must be dealt with quickly and decisively. And please don't forget that the Lord is explaining the fuller implications of the sixth commandment, therefore, following these simple rules would not only demonstrate us to be children of God and citizens of His kingdom, but it would prevent the hurts and squabbles of life from turning into the bitterness from which springs the strife, the estrangement, the division, and the destruction that ultimately leads to homicide. So important is this principle that even worship (i.e., sacrifice) bows before it. In other words: "[I]f you bring your gift to the altar, and there remember that your brother has something against you, leave your gift there before the altar, and go your way. First be reconciled to your brother, and then come and offer your gift." Not only would the world be a better place by the living out of this ethic, but the church would finally be what it was designed to be—a body of believers that truly love God and each other.

Matthew 5:27-30 "You have heard that it was said to those of old, 'You shall not commit adultery.' But I say to you that whoever looks at a woman to lust for her has already committed adultery with her in his heart. If your right eye causes you to sin, pluck it out and cast it from you; for it is more profitable for you that one of your members perish, than for your whole body to be cast into hell. And if your right hand causes you to sin, cut it off and cast it from you; for it is more profitable for you that one of your members perish, than for your whole body to be cast into hell."

Jesus now addresses the seventh commandment. What the people had heard was correct, but the implications of this commandment had not been explained. Jesus now plumbs the depth of this law to arrive at the heart of the matter.

Adultery, by definition, is sexual intercourse with someone else's spouse. But just like He did with the sixth commandment, Jesus reflects on the entire scope of adultery to include the imagination of the heart as well as the deed. Not only should the child of God not commit adultery, he ought not to even think it. Of course, Jesus is not saying sexual desire is inherently sinful. What He's saying is that whenever desire is satisfied, whether in thought or deed, with someone else's spouse, sin has occurred. Therefore, the child of God fights adultery where it begins—in the thoughts and intents of the heart.

Although what Jesus says in verses 29 and 30 has been interpreted by some as a literal call to self-mutilation, I know of no New Testament Christian who takes this position (Origen cited this verse, along with Matthew 19:12, as justification for castrating himself). To interpret what Jesus says here to be a reference to literal mutilation does nothing to explain what He's really talking about, for it cannot be doubted that a blind man with no hands can still lust in his heart for that which is unlawful for him to have. Remember, it is the inner man, and not the body, to which the Lord addresses Himself. He uses hyperbole to emphasize the drastic call the law against adultery makes to sever anything, and everything, that stimulates unholy desire. By denying illicit desire (viz., by figuratively plucking out an eye or cutting off a hand), children of God are not handicapping themselves. Instead, they are fitting themselves for the kingdom of God.

Matthew 5:31-32 "Furthermore it has been said, 'Whoever divorces his wife, let him give her a certificate of divorce.' But I say to you that whoever divorces his wife for any reason except sexual immorality causes her to commit adultery; and whoever marries a woman who is divorced commits adultery. "

What is said here ought to be studied along with what Jesus says in Matthew 19:3-9. The essence of Jesus' teaching on marriage, divorce and remarriage is that if two people are divorced on grounds other than adultery, and if they marry another, they are guilty of adultery. Many have come to think the words of Jesus here are a modification of "the law and the prophets," but let's examine this matter more closely.

Under the Law of Moses, there was legislation permitting divorce:

When a man takes a wife and marries her, and it happens that she finds no favor in his eyes because he has found some uncleanness in her, and he writes her a certificate of divorce, puts it in her hand, and sends her out of his house, when she has departed from his house, and goes and becomes another man's wife, if the latter husband detests her and writes her a certificate of divorce, puts it in her hand, and sends her out of his house, or if the latter husband dies who took her as his wife, then her former husband who divorced her must not take her back to be his wife after she has been defiled; for that is an abomination before the LORD, and you shall not bring sin on the land which the LORD your God is giving you as an inheritance.[27]

It must be understood that this concession of Moses was made due to the hardness of their hearts, according to Matthew 19:9. In other words, Deuteronomy 24:1-4 was not enacted to reflect a change in God's moral intention concerning marriage, which had, from the beginning, involved one man and one woman for life.[28] Giving a writing of divorcement was enacted to avert a greater evil, for without such legislation a man might unmercifully treat a wife in whom he had found "some uncleanness," even to the point of permanently injuring or killing her. Some say, "but this is ridiculous, as death was the Law's punishment for adultery." Yes, it was, but where do we find it being enforced by these hard-hearted Jews? Even today, adulterers still deserve death, but there are few courts, and perhaps even fewer Christians, who would seek to exact such a "harsh" punishment. Why? Because of the hardness of our hearts, of course. We simply do not see adultery, even the kind that takes place in our hearts, as the horrendous sin it really is, for many who call themselves after Christ attempt to justify the harboring of such unholy desires in their hearts as perfectly human and therefore natural. Only when we see this sin as God sees it will we be able to understand there has always been only one reason given by God to sever the divinely ordained relationship of marriage—namely, adultery on the part of one of the parties.

---

[27] Deut. 24:1-4.
[28] See Matt. 19:4-6.

However, because capital punishment required a certain judicial procedure in order to assure justice was being done, and because of the hardness of their hearts no one really pursued such justice, and because the sinned against party in the case of adultery was not permitted to take justice into his own hands, as such was proscribed by God's Law, he was to write her a "certificate of divorce" and "put it in her hand" before sending her away. Therefore, the only grounds God has sanctioned for putting one's mate away is "some uncleanness," which must be, if I've interpreted this correctly, adultery. This is why Jesus says that putting one's spouse away for any reason "except sexual immorality" (here in verse 32 and 19:9), puts both husband and wife in jeopardy of committing adultery, as both would be committing adultery when they joined themselves to another after being "legally" (in the sight of man) but not "scripturally" (in the sight of God) divorced.

The Jews had wrongly interpreted Deuteronomy 24:1-4 to be saying a man could put his spouse away "for just any reason" (19:3). According to these scribes and Pharisees, a certificate of divorce, no matter what the cause, dissolved the marriage in the eyes of God. Consequently, they taught that if one secured a legal document, he could put his wife away and marry another whenever he wanted. They were wrong in both assumptions, and the end result was what can only be called "legalized adultery." In fact, this was exactly the position of the School of Hillel, which declared it a sufficient grounds for divorce if the wife had spoiled her husband's dinner. Josephus, himself a two-time divorcé, had this to say about it: "He that desires to be divorced from his wife *for any cause whatsoever* (and many such causes happen among men), let him in writing give assurance that he will never use her again as his wife any more; for by this means she may be at liberty to marry another husband, although before this bill of divorce be given, she is not to be permitted so to do."[29]

So, it is just this kind of thinking Jesus was attempting to correct. (It is noteworthy that when Jehovah spoke of writing Israel

---

[29] *Antiquities*, IV, viii, 23.

a certificate of divorcement [cf. Jeremiah 3:8], it was for the nation's spiritual adultery, not because He was simply displeased with something they had done. And in Matthew 1:19, Joseph was going to put Mary away for what he thought, at the time, was her apparent adultery.) No, Moses did not permit divorce and remarriage *for just any cause*—the only cause, then and now, is adultery. This is what Jesus clearly teaches here in this Sermon on the Mount, hence, it is wrong to interpret these sayings as something new and revolutionary.

With this in mind, let's consider what the prophet Malachi said:

> And this is the second thing you do: You cover the altar of the LORD with tears, with weeping and crying; so He does not regard the offering anymore, nor receive it with goodwill from your hands. Yet you say, "For what reason?" Because the LORD has been witness between you and the wife of your youth, with whom you have dealt treacherously; yet she is your companion and your wife by covenant.... Therefore take heed to your spirit, and let none deal treacherously with the wife of his youth. For the LORD God of Israel says that He hates divorce, for it covers one's garment with violence, says the LORD of hosts. Therefore take heed to your spirit, that you do not deal treacherously.[30]

Notice that Jehovah's complaint was not that they were adulterers because they had failed to go through the formalities of a divorce. It was the divorcing and remarrying that God hated. Observe further that even though a divorce had been given, and we have to assume this was for every reason other than adultery, the put away woman was still the wife by covenant. Therefore, it is clear that the prophets taught that "legalized divorce" (viz., divorce "for just any cause") did not morally permit remarriage. So, once again, it is correct to say that Jesus and the prophets are agreed in their interpretation of the divorce concession of

---

[30] Mal. 2:13-16.

Deuteronomy 24. Moses' Law did not grant divorce and remarriage for just any cause, and those who so used it were guilty of "legalized adultery." Therefore, in Matthew 5:31-32 and Matthew 19:3-9, Jesus states clearly God's will as it should have been understood by the Jews.

Matthew 5:33-37 "Again you have heard that it was said to those of old, 'You shall not swear falsely, but shall perform your oaths to the Lord.' But I say to you, do not swear at all: neither by heaven, for it is God's throne; nor by the earth, for it is His footstool; nor by Jerusalem, for it is the city of the great King. Nor shall you swear by your head, because you cannot make one hair white or black. But let your 'Yes' be 'Yes,' and your 'No,' 'No.' For whatever is more than these is from the evil one."

Those who refuse to take an oath today, and I have known more than a few Christians who take this position, assume two things in regard to this passage: (1) that verse 33 is a summary of the ancient law on oaths; and (2) that Jesus annuls that law by instituting an absolute injunction against all oath taking. To shore up their case, they cite James 5:12, which says, "But above all, my brethren, do not swear, either by heaven or by earth or with any other oath. But let your 'Yes,' be 'Yes,' and your 'No,' 'No,' lest you fall into judgment." However, this scripture must be viewed through the correct interpretation of Matthew 5:33-37, as James does not say more than his Master. Thus, it is unnecessary for us to deal with this passage directly.

Although verse 33 seems to convey an accurate summary of the Old Testament teaching on oaths,[31] Jesus is driving at something more. Rabbinic teaching claimed that although all oaths invoking the divine name were binding, oaths that substituted other things for the divine name were necessarily not. Therefore, according to the "righteousness of the scribes and Pharisees,"[32] if one swore by God he must perform his oath, but if one swore by heaven, earth,

[31] See Lev. 19:12; Num. 30:2; Deut. 23:21.
[32] See verse 20.

or Jerusalem, his oath was not obligatory. That this is the true object of Jesus' correction can be seen from His argument in verses 34-36. It was just the sort of shenanigans the Lord inveighed against in Matthew 23:16-22, which was His final public confrontation with the Pharisees. There He said:

> Woe to you, blind guides, who say, "Whoever swears by the temple, it is nothing; but whoever swears by the gold of the temple, he is obliged to perform it." Fools and blind! For which is greater, the gold or the temple that sanctifies the gold? And, "Whoever swears by the altar, it is nothing; but whoever swears by the gift that is on it, he is obliged to perform it." Fools and blind! For which is greater, the gift or the altar that sanctifies the gift? Therefore he who swears by the altar, swears by it and by all things on it. He who swears by the temple, swears by it and by Him who dwells in it. And he who swears by heaven, swears by the throne of God and by Him who sits on it.

Jews who had become so corrupt in their day to day lives and businesses were wont to swear often as they tried to deceive others into thinking they were being honest. Their surreptitious substitution of the name of God in their oaths was nothing more than a cover for their cheating and lying. What hypocrites these Jews were. As God's children, they should have been totally honest, and so much so that their *yeas* and *nays* could be taken on face value. But this was not the sort of people with which Jesus dealt in the Sermon on the Mount. Their "righteousness" was so pathetic that, without repentance, they could not be part of God's glorious kingdom. No wonder Jesus warned His disciples to beware of the leaven of the Pharisees,[33] for their hypocrisy, which was the hidden, penetrating motivation in their lives, had totally corrupted them, causing them to stray far from that heartfelt obedience that is the sign of true religion to one of pure pretense.[34] The Talmud contained an entire section, called *Shebuoth*, that codified the

---

[33] See Matt. 16:6; Mk. 8:15.
[34] See Lk. 12:1.

rabbinic hairsplitting on oaths that taught swearing *by* Jerusalem was not binding, but swearing while facing *toward* Jerusalem was. Consequently, it should not be hard for one to understand that Jesus was not here critiquing the teaching of the law and prophets in regard to oaths, but the rabbinic perversions that had come to be accepted by the Jews.

In addition, to argue from these verses that Jesus unqualifiedly prohibited all oaths is to ignore the fact that Jesus Himself answered under oath[35] and that solemn oaths were invoked by the apostle Paul on several different occasions.[36] These examples evidence that not all oaths, in which an appeal to God as witness is made, are prohibited by what Jesus said here. But didn't Jesus say, "Swear not at all"? Yes, He certainly did, but such language must be interpreted in view of everything that has been said so far. Commenting on this, John Murray wrote:

> We are not violating good and necessary principles of interpretation if we regard the word of Jesus, "Swear not at all," thought absolute in its terms, as having reference simply to the kind of profanity with which He was expressly dealing, the disguised swearing of which Jesus proceeds forthwith to give examples. In other words, if we infer that what Jesus unreservedly prohibits is the subterfuge with which He is expressly dealing, namely, the surreptitious use of terms which have a Godward reference on the supposition that thereby we get away from profane and false swearing, then we have not only an acceptable but sufficient interpretation of the prohibition, "Swear not at all."

Murray, I think, is precisely right in his interpretation, and besides, any other interpretation has Jesus annulling the Law, which has Him contradicting what He said in Matthew 5:17, which was: "Do not think that I came to destroy the Law or the Prophets. I did not come to destroy but to fulfill."

---

[35] See Matt. 26:63-64.
[36] See Rom. 1:19; 2 Cor. 1:23; Gal. 1:20; Phil. 1:8; 1 Thess. 1:10; 2:5.

Matthew 5:38-42 "You have heard that it was said, 'An eye for an eye and a tooth for a tooth.' But I tell you not to resist an evil person. But whoever slaps you on your right cheek, turn the other to him also. If anyone wants to sue you and take away your tunic, let him have your cloak also. And whoever compels you to go one mile, go with him two. Give to him who asks you, and from him who wants to borrow from you do not turn away."

Since Jesus mentions the "eye for an eye" principle, which was taught in the Law of Moses,[37] and counters it with instruction not to resist one who is evil, it is assumed by many that Jesus is here contrasting the Old Covenant with what will become His New Testament. This is wrong. The "eye for an eye" principle, or *lex talionis*, as it is sometimes called, represents a sound judicial principle that all courts should follow. It says, simply, that punishment should be commensurate with the crime committed. That is, the punishment for murder and the punishment for speeding cannot be the same and be consistent with this principle. This law was meant as a judicial restraint, not a guide for personal vindication. But the rabbinic tradition had turned it into the latter. Therefore, the very law that provided for evenhanded justice and prohibited the spirit of revenge that stokes the fires of feuds and vendettas had been misappropriated by the Jews to validate all those things the law was designed to prohibit. So, something intended only for the court had been applied to the Jews' personal ethic, permitting them to extract their own "justice" without the benefit of due process of law; the very idea this commandment was designed to prohibit.

Consequently, the contrast Jesus is making here is between what the law actually required and what rabbinic tradition permitted. Addressing, then, the subject of personal ethics, which was the thing that had been perverted by the rabbinic tradition, Jesus says "resist not an evil person." The Greek word translated "resist" is *anthistemi*, and it means "to stand against, oppose,

---

[37] See Ex. 21:23; Lev. 24:17-21.

withstand." But just as we learned that "swear not at all" was not absolute but qualified, it ought not to be thought surprising that "resist not an evil person" is also not absolute but qualified. But before proceeding further with these qualifications, I think it would be helpful to notice what the end result is of the teaching of those who believe Jesus is annulling the Old Testament with an absolute (i.e., unqualified) commandment that applies not just to personal ethics, but to the judicial system as well.

Writing from a Mennonite viewpoint, Guy Franklin Hershberger says:

> When Jesus set aside the civil law of eye for eye and tooth for tooth, He was not speaking of personal retaliation, but of the ordinary legal method of avenging a wrong. Even the Mosaic code did not permit an individual who had lost a tooth to strike out the tooth of the offender personally. He must rather report the offense to the civil authorities and then the magistrates would administer punishment, which might consist of removing the offender's tooth. [Notice that Hershberger acknowledges here that the Law of Moses did not permit personal vendettas.] In Matthew 5:38, therefore, Jesus is saying that Christians must not appeal to the state for revenge against offenders.[38]

Those who agree with Hershberger—and I think at least some of my pacifist brethren do—must consider immoral what would otherwise be described as justice. So let's see how this interpretation translates into real life. Picture a court scene where the victim is bandaged heavily on the right side of his head. On the other side of the courtroom is the defendant, unrepentant and arrogant. At the end of the trial, the judge orders the victim to turn his head so the defendant can strike him on his left side. After this sentence is duly executed, the victim is taken to the hospital while the defendant is released. Justice? Absolutely not, and any nation that

---

[38] Hershberger, *War, Peace and Nonresistance*, p. 51.

practices such "justice" is headed straight for the pit.[39] Therefore, the radical pacifists' position cannot be correct.

But, if the Lord is contrasting the true morality of the Law with the "righteousness of the scribes and Pharisees,"[40] an entirely different light is cast upon His words. This was addressed by Arthur W. Pink in *An Exposition of the Sermon on the Mount*:

> The Divine statute...had been grossly perverted by the scribes and Pharisees. They had wrested its purpose and design by giving it a false application. Instead of confining it to the magistrates in the law courts, they had made the statute a promiscuous one. The Jewish leaders had so expounded this precept as though God had given permission for each individual to take the law into his own hands and to avenge his own wrongs. They intimated that it allowed each person to take private revenge upon his enemies; if thy neighbor smite thee and destroyeth one of thine eyes, then go thou and do likewise to him. Thus a spirit of resistance was cherished and the act of retaliation was condoned.[41]

Therefore, when Jesus said "resist not an evil person," He was specifically addressing the kind of thinking outlined above. He was not prohibiting the righteous exercise of judicial justice, but the exercise of personal revenge. Consequently, there was nothing wrong with the *lex talionis* (viz., the law of like for like) principle taught in the Law of Moses. In fact, it was, and still is, the model *par excellence* for earthly justice. However, such was not created as a personal set of ethics. It was created, instead, as a judicial remedy against personal vengeance—something that very seldom manifests the *weightier matters* of the law—things like mercy, justice and faith. Nevertheless, if all mankind were to live according to the principles articulated in the Sermon on the Mount, there would be no need for the mechanical remedies provided by civil authorities. But because mankind is fallen, Romans 13

---

[39] See Psa. 9:17; Prov. 14:34.
[40] See Matt. 5:20.
[41] Page 113.

governments, which are governments ordained by God, function as God-given ministers of Justice and Righteousness. Government authorities, even when they fail to realize it, and whether they like it or not, are subject to God's Law above the law and will answer to His "rod of iron" if their policies are contrary to His principles. And the degree to which a government finds this offensive is a good indicator of just how far down the path towards a Revelation 13 government, which is a government ordained by Satan, it has traveled.

Therefore, it ought to be absolutely clear that Jesus was not addressing His remarks to civil authorities, who had divine authorization to execute vengeance. Instead, He was addressing the common man and was, therefore, dealing *only* with personal ethics. As such, they were not new at all. Jesus' illustrations here reflect the disposition of the true child of God and are the most practical ever given to man. The individual who understands and implements this personal set of ethics will learn to cultivate the kind of life God created mankind to live from the very beginning.

When these illustrations are compared with other scriptures, one should be able to easily conclude that nonresistance to the evildoer is not without limitations. For example, the command to give away our coat and cloak, along with the injunction not to refuse him who would borrow from us, must be interpreted in light of other Scriptural obligations and duties.[42] Nothing Jesus said in these verses encouraged slothfulness, injustice or wickedness, and He certainly did not repudiate due process of law. However, even when due process is not available, for whatever reason, the child of God is not excused to do wrong by personally extracting an eye-for-an-eye and a tooth-for-a-tooth vengeance.

Matthew 5:43-48 "You have heard that it was said, 'You shall love your neighbor and hate your enemy.' But I say to you, love your enemies, bless those who curse you, do good to those who hate you, and pray for those who spitefully use you and persecute you, that you may be sons of your

---

[42] See 1 Tim. 5:8; 2 Thess. 3:6-12; 2 Jn. 10-11.

Father in heaven; for He makes His sun rise on the evil and on the good, and sends rain on the just and on the unjust. For if you love those who love you, what reward have you? Do not even the tax collectors do the same? And if you greet your brethren only, what do you do more than others? Do not even the tax collectors do so? Therefore you shall be perfect, just as your Father in heaven is perfect."

Now we come to the most fundamental and critical issue of what it means to be a true child of God. Because our Heavenly Father is a loving God, we too must be loving people. This section, more than any of the others we've looked at, establishes the fact that the Lord is countering misinterpretations of the Law of Moses, rather than refuting it. "You shall love your neighbor" was definitely from the Law of Moses,[43] but "hate your enemy" can't be found anywhere in the Old Testament. In fact, the Old Testament required the child of God to love his enemies.[44] However, the supposed right to hate one's enemies, which had been incorporated into the "righteousness of the scribes and Pharisees,"[45] probably derived from a false interpretation of Leviticus 19:17—an interpretation which incorrectly distinguished between a neighbor and an enemy. Although the Law of Moses had properly instructed the Jews about their treatment of "the stranger" or Gentile,[46] they incorrectly classified "enemy" to include any Gentile, and because the rabbinic tradition had wrongly taught them to hate their enemies, they therefore despised all Gentiles, even those who were closely related to the Jews, as were the Samaritans. The attitude Jesus is here addressing is understood by what Jesus said in Luke 10:25-37:

And behold, a certain lawyer stood up and tested Him, saying, "Teacher, what shall I do to inherit eternal life?" He said to him,

---

[43] See Lev. 19:17-18.
[44] See Ex. 23:4-5; Prov. 25:21,23; 24:17-18.
[45] Matt. 5:20.
[46] See Lev. 19:10, 33-34; 24:22; 25:35; Num. 15:16; Deut. 10:19.

"What is written in the law? What is your reading of it?" So he answered and said, "You shall love the LORD your God with all your heart, with all your soul, with all your strength, and with all your mind," and "your neighbor as yourself." And He said to him, "You have answered rightly; do this and you will live." But he, wanting to justify himself, said to Jesus, "And who is my neighbor?" Then Jesus answered and said: "A certain man went down from Jerusalem to Jericho, and fell among thieves, who stripped him of his clothing, wounded him, and departed, leaving him half dead. Now by chance a certain priest came down that road. And when he saw him, he passed by on the other side. Likewise a Levite, when he arrived at the place, came and looked, and passed by on the other side. But a certain Samaritan, as he journeyed, came where he was. And when he saw him, he had compassion. So he went to him and bandaged his wounds, pouring on oil and wine; and he set him on his own animal, brought him to an inn, and took care of him. On the next day, when he departed, he took out two denarii, gave them to the innkeeper, and said to him, "Take care of him; and whatever more you spend, when I come again, I will repay you." So which of these three do you think was neighbor to him who fell among the thieves? And he said, "He who showed mercy on him." Then Jesus said to him, "Go and do likewise."

In this passage, the Lord uses a hated Samaritan to teach what the Law had in view when it talked about one's responsibility to love his neighbor. The Jews hated the Samaritans so badly that when they resorted to name-calling, they not only called Jesus a "bastard,"[47] but a "demon possessed Samaritan," as well.[48] In their way of thinking, there wasn't anything much worse than a demon-filled Samaritan "bastard."[49] But the Samaritan Jesus mentions, motivated by compassion, rather than hate, demonstrated what loving one's neighbor was really all about. (Another

---

[47] See Jn. 8:41.

[48] See Jn. 8:48.

[49] I realize how crass this sounds, but sometimes we just need to come to grips with what the Bible actually says.

example of Jesus reflecting favorably on a Samaritan is found in Luke 17:15-19.) As human beings, there are none who are not our neighbors, and this is what the Law of Moses, when properly interpreted, taught—and this is what Jesus taught these Jews in His Sermon on the Mount treatise. He made it clear that, by their racist and haughty attitudes, they were violating their covenantal duties. Instead of hating their enemies, whoever they thought them to be, they should have been loving them, for their enemies, due to the fact that they too were created in the image of God, were their neighbors. Far from being part of a new and revolutionary ethic, this was precisely God's law under the Old Covenant, as it is today under the New Covenant. To hate those who hate and use us, who insult us, who sue us and force us into service against our wills, has never been hard, and it was this that made up the "righteousness of the scribes and Pharisees." But to love our enemies, that's the hard part; the narrow way that few are able to find. But it is in this narrow path that the children of God walk. Jim McGuiggan, on page 10 of his excellent little book, *The God of the Towel,* comments on this kind of love by reflecting on the perfection of God's love, a love that causes it to rain on both the just and the unjust: *"His is no 'if' love (I'll love you if you do what I say!). His is more than 'because' love (I love you because...). His is an 'anyway' love (I love you no matter how you are!)."* It is this equality of God's love that is such a big part of what God being "perfect" is all about. Therefore, it should not surprise us that children of God are called upon to be perfect just as our Father in heaven is perfect.[50]

Conclusion

This rather lengthy soliloquy was undertaken to demonstrate that the several contrasts made in Jesus' Sermon on the Mount were actually between the true morality prescribed in the Law of Moses and the so-called "righteousness of the scribes and

---

[50] See Matt. 5:48.

Pharisees"—a "righteousness" based on perverted interpretations and misapplications of the Law itself. If my premise has been demonstrated to be true, and I believe it has, then Jesus' sayings here are to be viewed in an entirely different light than pacifists have viewed them. This is not a new set of ethics reserved just for the Christian age, but represents the morality contained in the Law of Moses as well as Christianity. Therefore, just as "swear not at all" was qualified by permitted oaths under the Law of Moses, so was "resist not an evil person," for under the law of Moses an evil person was to be punished by the judicial system, not the individual, so that justice might be done.

The basis for this set of ethics or morality, of course, is nothing less than the eternal character of God. His inherent goodness determines whether something is right or wrong, and since the eternal character of God does not change,[51] the status of moral principles remains the same in every Bible age. The Sermon on the Mount serves to demonstrate that there is a continuity of Biblical ethics that is ignored by pacifist exegetes. It is this continuity that has New Testament writers citing Old Testament passages when speaking of moral duties.[52] The morality of Moses' Law cannot be surpassed, therefore, moral duties under both the Old and New covenants are not totally dissimilar, as the radical pacifists contend. A Jew who functioned officially as an executor of God's wrath under the Law of Moses was under obligation, in his personal set of ethics, to love his enemy and not resist an evil person, just as Christians are today. Therefore, just as it was true that those who administered the sword under the Law of Moses could do so without violating their personal obligation not to take the law into their own hands, so Christians today who function as sword bearers do not incur guilt when they inflict punishment or death in the God-ordained pursuit of Justice and Righteousness.

In His Sermon on the Mount, the Lord tells us what true religion is all about—and by "true religion" I mean religion

---

[51] See Mal. 3:6; Jas. 1:17.
[52] See Rom. 12:19-20; 13:9-10; Jas. 2:8, 11.

unencumbered by the think-sos of men. It calls us to the highest standard of practical, spiritual living, and the one who practices its precepts and principles will be in a position to "prove" to a lost and dying world "what is that good and acceptable and perfect will of God."[53] But we must not become careless, as some have, thinking that this sermon is an exhaustive or complete set of personal and social ethics.[54] Although the Lord's sermon explicates many moral responsibilities, it does not encompass all of them. Generally speaking, it discusses person to person relationships, therefore, many social duties and ethical predicaments will arise in life that Jesus did not here discuss. For example, civil government's role in achieving social justice is not examined in the Sermon on the Mount, not because it would no longer be sanctioned,[55] but because it was not the subject of the Lord's attention. It is perfectly reasonable, and therefore legitimate, to think He thought civil government would continue praising good and punishing evil, just as it was commissioned to do under the Law of Moses. That this interpretation is correct is proved by Romans 13:1-7, where an apostle of Christ sets forth the function of civil government under the New Testament which, because of the Lord's mandate of the separation of church and state,[56] no longer exacts punishment for purely religious offenses, as the courts did under the theocracy of the Old Testament.

Unfortunately, and as it applies to the issue before us, radical pacifists, just like the scribes and Pharisees to whom Jesus addressed His sermon, have so misinterpreted and misapplied the Lord's sermon that they are now more than willing to condemn the guiltless, just as their religious forefathers did in Jesus' time.[57]

In the next chapter, we'll examine "The Warrior's Burden."

---

[53] Rom. 12:2b.
[54] I call this "bumper sticker morality."
[55] See Rom. 13:1-7.
[56] See Matt. 22:21.
[57] See Matt. 12:7.

Chapter 6

The Warrior's Burden (Part 1): The Psychological And Spiritual Ramifications Of Killing

In 1 Chronicles 22:8, David said to Solomon, "My son, as for me, it was in my mind to build a house to the name of the Lord my God; but the word of the Lord came to me, saying, 'You have shed much blood and have made great wars; you shall not build a house for My name, because you have shed much blood on the earth in My sight.'" Later, when David assembled all the leaders of Israel in Jerusalem, he told them that it had been in his mind to build a "house of rest for the ark of the covenant of the Lord, and for the footstool of our God," and had even made preparations to do so when the Lord stopped him by saying, "You shall not build a house for My name, because you have been a man of war, and have shed blood."[1] These statements have been used by many religionists to teach that the shedding of blood in war somehow taints a servant of God. But such is a fundamental misunderstanding of these scriptures, for the Bible, in these passages and elsewhere, teaches no such doctrine.

King David was kept busy most of his life with war-fighting duties. But toward the end of his life, he secured the peace, with God's help, and Israel enjoyed relative rest from her enemies.

---

[1] 1 Chron. 28:2-3.

During this time, David desired to build a house for the Lord. He was even encouraged in this by God through the prophet Nathan, who said, "Go, do all that is in your heart, for the Lord is with you."[2] However, the Lord makes it clear to David that it will be his son, and not him, who will build the Temple.[3] The context makes it clear that David's war-fighting tasks had left him no time for building the Lord's house, but Solomon, who would inherit the peace his father had won for him and the nation, would be able to undertake the task of building the temple of God in Jerusalem. This is exactly the way Solomon interpreted what his father had told him, for when speaking with Hiram, king of Tyre, he said:

> You know how my father David could not build a house for the name of the Lord his God because of the wars which were fought against him on every side, until the Lord put his foes under the soles of his feet. But now the Lord my God has given me rest on every side, so that there is neither adversary nor evil occurrence. And behold, I propose to build a house for the name of the Lord my God, as the Lord spoke to my father David, saying, "Your son, whom I will set on your throne in your place, he shall build the house for My name."[4]

David's lot was not to build the Lord's house in Jerusalem. It was to defeat Israel's enemies so that his son would have the time and opportunity to do so. This is all the Bible is saying, and to impugn or demean David's war-fighting responsibilities as somehow being inferior to Solomon's task of building God's house is to seriously misinterpret God's word and imbibe the religious elitism that relegates war-fighting tasks to all other dirty-hands (i.e., sinful) activity. In truth, without David's valuable war-fighting contribution, Solomon would have had neither the time nor the opportunity to build God's Temple. Consequently, the shedding of blood in war is not inherently evil, as many suppose. Instead, and

---

[2] 2 Sam. 7:3.
[3] See 2 Sam. 7:12.
[4] I Ki. 5:3-5.

as long as such killing is done righteously, it is an invaluable contribution to one's neighbor and , as such, a personification of that neighborly love prescribed so many places in God's word. Furthermore, as the work of war encompasses the possibility of being killed as much as it does the possibility of killing, it jibes perfectly with the Lord's saying that "Greater love has no one than this, than to lay down one's life for his friends."[5]

Consequently, the task of war-fighting, as long as it is done consistent with the principles of justice and righteousness taught in God's word, is an honorable, God-given duty that personifies the essence of godly love. Under these conditions, the soldierly task is no more dishonorable than marriage, which the Bible, contrary to Roman Catholic doctrine, describes as "honorable."[6] In fact, killing in war, as long as it is done under the circumstances mentioned above, is no more impure and defiled than is sexual intercourse performed within the confines of marriage. Religionists down through two millennia of Christendom (particularly the Romanists) have frequently disparaged both marriage and war by claiming that those who participate in these two God-given endeavors are, if not outright sinners, at least less spiritual than those who keep themselves from such things.

It is most unfortunate, then, that the presumption-of-guilt theories that have been manifested by many religionists concerning the sinfulness of war function as added burdens to be heaped on the already overloaded shoulders of warriors who are duty bound, when necessary, to take human life. These religionists, in their self-righteousness, are blinded to their own unholy criticism—criticism that says all war-fighting, like all other such dirty-hands tasks, are to be left to those who are already sinners. This sentiment, all too prevalent in the so-called "Christian" West, has been a bane to righteous war-fighting.

As a result, soldiers in the West experiencing the very real and profound trauma of combat have been further traumatized by the

---

[5] Jn. 15:13.
[6] Heb. 13:4.

ever present religious perspective that views all killing, even that which is done in the pursuit of justice and righteousness, as sinful. This is, to be as succinct as I know how to be, downright shameful, and is audacious elitism at its very worst. Is it any wonder, then, that soldiers in the West, who in modern times have been, by far, the morally cleanest warriors, have experienced a disproportionate number of the medical and psychological problems that have come to be known as post-traumatic stress disorder (PTSD)?

Man's Innate Resistance To Killing

There can be no doubt that war-fighting exacts a toll on those who engage in it. Man, it seems, has a strong resistance to killing his fellow man. This resistance appears to be universal and innate (i.e., God-given). Studies have shown that when faced with the prospect of killing another human being, many have been unable to do so. This is true even in those cases where the one refusing to kill faced grave bodily harm or even death.

That this is true ought not to be all that hard for Christians to understand, for we see ourselves as creatures made in the image of God. As such, we view God as our heavenly Father and our fellow human beings as brothers and sisters. This view sees mankind as a family, and it is hard to kill our relatives. This strong resistance to killing is nothing to be ashamed of. In fact, it ought to be relished by every right-thinking person. But when soldiers who have been influenced by the anti-war ideas so prevalent in the "Christian" West entertain the idea that warfare, by its very nature, is tainted with sin (i.e., killing is always wrong, no matter what), they become prime candidates ("sitting ducks," if you will) for serious spiritual and psychological problems. It is to these pathologies that I now direct your attention.

Fight Or Flight

Some years back, I remember watching a Civil War reenactment where the "Yankees" and "Rebs" stood firing at each other in an open space separated by not more than thirty yards. I remember the thought of these two units approaching each other, stopping, firing their first thunderous volleys, reloading, firing again, and all this while men on both sides were falling wounded or dead. I asked the "Colonel" who was in charge about this and he told me that if a soldier didn't break and run after the first volley, he would usually stand and fight "all day." What the Colonel was describing was the well-known "fight-or-flight" reaction articulated by modern psychology and enthroned by military science. This model says that in the face of danger a series of physiological and psychological processes prepare the individual to either stand and fight or run away. However, it has more recently been documented that such a model does not accurately describe the actuality of combat. There is more to it than that, as Richard Heckler has pointed out:

> The notion that the only alternatives to conflict are fight and flight are embedded in our culture, and our educational institutions have done little to challenge it. The traditional American military policy raises it to the level of a law of nature.[7]

As Lt. Col. David Grossman wrote on page 5 of his Pulitzer-prize nominated 1995 book, entitled *On Killing: The Psychological Costs of Learning to Kill in War and Society*:

> The fight-or-flight dichotomy is the appropriate set of choices for any creature faced with danger *other* than that which comes from its own species. [But] When we examine the responses of creatures confronted with aggression from their own species, the set of options expands to include posturing and submission. This application of animal kingdom intraspecies response patterns (that is, fight, flee, posture, and submit) to human warfare is, to the best of my knowledge, entirely new.

The *fight-flee-posture-submit* model is not only new, but is, when used to examine the history of war-fighting by American

---

[7] *In Search of the Warrior Spirit*, 1989, North Atlantic Books.

soldiers, quite revealing. According to Grossman and other researchers, it has been discovered that, until fairly recently, few American soldiers who participated in combat actually tried to kill the enemy. Up to and including World War II, it was believed that a soldier would kill the enemy because his country and leaders asked him to do so and because of his desire to save his own life and the lives of his friends. But in U.S. Army Brigadier General S. L. A. Marshall's pioneering work, *Men Against Fire*, which was published in 1978, it was unexpectedly discovered that only 15 to 20 out of every 100 combat soldiers questioned about what they did in battle actually admitted to firing their weapons at the enemy. He found this was true "whether the action was spread over a day, or two days or three." These astounding figures were not just anecdotal but were based on individual and mass interviews with thousands of soldiers in more than four hundred infantry companies, in Europe and the Pacific, immediately after they had been in close combat with German or Japanese units.

In a footnote on page 333, Grossman mentions that the quality of Marshall's research has been questioned by some. However, Marshall's findings, he says, have been corroborated by his own research, as well as that of others. Therefore, it is shocking to learn that only 15 to 20 percent of American riflemen actually fired at the enemy. However, and contrary to what you may be thinking, there is nothing in this research that indicates these soldiers were cowards. On the contrary, those who would not fire did not run away or hide, as it might, at first, be assumed. In fact, they were, in many cases, willing to risk grave bodily harm to rescue fellow soldiers, get ammunition, or run messages. But when all was said and done, they simply would not fire their weapons at the enemy, even when faced with the enemy's repeated assaults. But mounting research has demonstrated that these figures are not just indicative of soldiers who made up America's "Greatest Generation," but actually hold true of all wars Americans had fought before the Korean War.

The Example Of The Civil War

I am a bit of a Civil War[8] buff. In the reading I've done, I have always wondered why more soldiers were not killed or wounded during the Civil War. When one takes into consideration the capacity of the weapons used and the fact that the average distance in battle between units in that war was thirty yards, it seems clear that many more should have been killed or wounded than were. After all, the Civil War weapon of choice was a muzzle-loading, black-powder, rifled musket that in order to be fired required its possessor to take a paper-wrapped cartridge consisting of a bullet and some gunpowder that then had to be torn with the loader's teeth. He poured the powder down the barrel, set the bullet (usually a .58 caliber) in the barrel, rammed it home, primed the weapon with a percussion cap, cocked it, and fired. Because gravity was necessary to pour the powder down the barrel, all of this was done from an exposed, standing position. These weapons were fast and accurate for their day and could be fired at the rate of four or five shots a minute. So, because fighting was usually done from a standing position (again, at an average distance of thirty yards), it seems clear that if most Civil War combatants had been actively involved in trying to kill or wound the enemy, more soldiers (Blue and Gray) should have died during those four long years of war.

But instead of mowing down hundreds of enemy soldiers during the first minutes of such engagements, the regiments involved killed only one or two men per minute. When one considers that, instead of quickly disintegrating in a hail of lead, these opposing units stood and exchanged fire for hours on end, it is truly amazing there were not more casualties.[9] But after a while (and sometimes sooner), these engaged units would begin to break down.

---

[8] Actually, I prefer to call that terrible 4-year war the "War of Northern Aggression," but that is, perhaps, another story for another time.

[9] As wars go, the Civil War was the bloodiest in our history, with at least 618,000 dead. However, only slightly more than 204,000 were deaths resulting from battle. The rest were from disease and other such impediments.

And in the resulting "fog of war," the confusion, the smoke, the thunder of the firing, and the screams of the wounded would cause the soldiers to revert from their function as cogs in a finely-oiled military machine to individuals doing what only comes naturally. As Grossman points out, "Some load, some pass weapons, some tend the wounded, some shout orders, a few run, a few wander off in the smoke and find a convenient low spot to sink into, and a few, a very few, shoot"[10] In other words, the popular notion of a line of Civil War soldiers standing in formation and firing at the enemy until one side or the other is defeated appears not to be true and is borne out by the following description of the Battle of Antietam by one who participated in it:

> Now is the pinch. Men and officers...are fused into a common mass, in the frantic struggle to shoot fast. Everybody tears cartridges, loads, passes guns, or shoots. Men are falling in their places or running back into the corn."[11]

This is an image of battle that appears over and over again. In this account and Marshall's World War II research, we learn that only a few men actually shoot at the enemy, while others gather and prepare ammo, load weapons, pass weapons, or fall back into the obscurity and anonymity of cover.

Posturing And The Plague Of "Firing High"

According to Grossman, when a man is frightened, "he literally stops thinking with his forebrain (that is, with the mind of a human being) and starts to think with the midbrain (namely, the portion of his brain that is essentially indistinguishable from that of an animal), and in the mind of an animal it is the one who makes the loudest noise or puffs himself up the largest who will

---

[10] Grossman, *p. 20.*
[11] P. Griffith, *Battle Tactics of the Civil War,* 1989.

win."[12] So, with the advent of gunpowder, soldiers who were reluctant to kill were provided the ultimate tool for posturing. Instead of fleeing the battlefield in disgrace, gunpowder weapons provided the soldier who was reluctant to fire at the enemy with an instrument (notice that I did not say "weapon") that would satisfy his deep-seated need to posture while he, in turn, fired harmlessly over the heads of his enemy. The soldiers doing this—evidently the majority, if Grossman and others are correct—were indistinguishable from the few who were actually firing at the enemy with intent to kill or injure him.

So, with the advent of gunpowder, many soldiers who remained adamantly resistant to killing on the battlefield, were provided a means whereby they did not have to personally kill anyone (i.e., they simply postured, firing over the heads of the enemy). Because their doing so could not be distinguished from those few who were actually shooting to wound or kill, they did not have to experience the shame of being called cowards. This, therefore, provided the perfect opportunity for the 80-85 percent non-firers that recent research has uncovered. Assuming, as I think we now should, that man has always had this resistance, why would the history of thousands of years not tell us so? Simply this: *it is the victors who write the history books.* In other words, those who are good at killing in war are the very ones who frequently fight and claw their way to the top, in the military as well as in the political sphere. In fact, the great military leaders of millennia past have frequently become the successful political leaders of their people and nations. Therefore, if it has been true that for thousands of years the vast majority of soldiers, secretly and privately, were less than enthusiastic about killing their fellowman on the battlefield, the professional soldiers and their chroniclers would not be very open and candid about the inabilities of those under their tutelage. Consequently, military history, or at least a good portion of it, is surely written to shore up the military's authority and avoid, at least, the

---

[12] Grossman, p. 8.

revealing of its "weakness, vacillation, or distemper."[13] Add to this the fact that the media have done much to perpetuate the myth of easy killing, depicting its James Bonds, Luke Skywalkers, Rambos, and Indiana Joneses as casually and remorselessly killing off men by the hundreds, and it should come as little surprise that there has been so much disinformation about the true nature of killing one's fellowman. But by the time of the Korean War, a pronounced breakdown of this resistance began to manifest itself, with the firing rate increased to 55 percent (cf. Marshall's study). By the time of the Vietnam War, this rate had been increased to an amazing 90-95 percent (cf. Scott's study). What powerful tool was implemented to bring about this profound difference?

Operant Conditioning

The answer is *operant conditioning* or "programming," as veterans have frequently called it. Ivan P. Pavlov's experiments with dogs and B. F. Skinner's with rats taught us that animals, as well as man, can be taught to produce certain kinds of conditioned reflexes. The modern soldier, unlike soldiers of the past, is no longer taught to just be brave and fight well, he is aggressively conditioned from boot camp on to "engage" (the standard military euphemism for "kill") the enemy. Listen to how Grossman explains it:

> The method used to train today's—and Vietnam era's—U. S. Army and USMC soldiers is nothing more than an application of conditioning techniques to develop a reflexive "quick shoot" ability.... In my two decades of military service not a single soldier, sergeant, or officer, nor a single official or unofficial reference, has communicated an understanding that conditioning was occurring during marksmanship training. But from the standpoint of a psychologist who is also a historian and a career soldier, it has become

---

[13] Alfred Vagts, *A History of Militarism.*

increasingly obvious to me that this is exactly what has been achieved.

Instead of lying prone on a green grassy field calmly shooting at a bull's-eye target, the modern soldier spends many hours standing in a foxhole, with full combat equipment draped about his body, looking over an area of lightly wooded rolling terrain. At periodic intervals one or two olive-drab, man-shaped targets at varying ranges will pop up in front of him for a brief time, and the soldier must instantly aim and shoot at the target(s). When he hits a target it provides immediate feedback by instantly and very satisfyingly dropping backwards—just as a living target would. Soldiers are highly rewarded and recognized for success in this skill and suffer mild punishment (in the form of retraining, peer pressure, and failure to graduate from boot camp) for failure to quickly and accurately "engage" the targets—a standard euphuism for "kill."

In addition to traditional marksmanship, what is being taught in this environment is the ability to shoot reflexively and instantly and a precise mimicry of the act of killing on the modern battlefield. In behavioral terms, the man shape [targets] popping up in the soldier's field of fire is the "conditional stimulus," the immediate engaging of the target is the "target behavior." "Positive reinforcement" is given in the form of immediate feedback when the target drops when it is hit. In a form of "token economy" these hits are then exchanged for marksmanship badges that usually have some form of privilege or reward (praise, public recognition, three-day passes, and so on) associated with them.

Every aspect of killing on the battlefield is rehearsed, visualized, and conditioned. On special occasions even more realistic and complex targets are used.... These make the training more interesting, the conditioned stimuli more realistic, and the conditioned response more assured under a variety of different circumstances...

...This is all common practice in most of the world's best armies. Most modern infantry leaders understand that realistic training with immediate feedback to the soldier works, and they know that it is essential for success and survival on the modern battlefield....

What makes this training process work is the same thing that made Pavlov's dogs salivate and B. F. Skinner's rats press their bars. What makes it work is the single most powerful and reliable

behavior modification process yet discovered by the field of psychology, and now applied to the field of warfare: operant conditioning.[14]

So, with the rise of modern training in warfare there came the
desired increase in the average soldier's willingness to kill the enemy. Instead of the 15-20 percent firing rate of bygone years, soldiers who are willing to wound and kill the enemy has risen to
90-95 percent. This has made the American military—when unrestrained by the incessant political hamstringing that is always associated with the use of military force—the most efficient,
effective, and awesome killing machine on the face of the earth.

As recent history has demonstrated, there is little room to
doubt that, on the battlefield, American military force is simply
unmatched. It has both the ability and the will to kill more enemy
combatants than any army in modern history. At the same time,
the American military is, by far, the most humane fighting machine ever assembled. With its so-called "smart weapons," it actively pursues a policy to kill as few non-combatants as feasible.

(There is, of course, a real vulnerability inherent in such behavior—a vulnerability that was exploited by the Communists in
Vietnam and now by the Muslim insurgents/guerrillas in Iraq.
The latter purposefully use populated areas as sanctuaries that
shield them from an all-out attack by coalition forces. They hide
behind non-combatants [men, women, and children] as they do
their dirty work, unable and unwilling to engage the Americans *et
al.* head on. When coalition forces are finally forced to clean these
strongholds out, the media characteristically dwell on the civilians [especially women and children] who are regrettably killed
and injured in these assaults. American soldiers are doing a mar-
velous job under these circumstances. As they go into harm's way,
they need to know that they are doing the right thing by not engaging in the wholesale killing that other, less-restrained, armies
would no doubt engage in, even though such restraint obviously

---

[14] Grossman, pp. 253-254.

places them in greater personal danger than if they simply "pounded the rubble," as some have suggested. Instead, they are subjected to a constant barrage of bad-mouthing of these efforts that comes from their elected leaders back home. As we'll see, this just heaps more psychological baggage on the shoulders of those who are already carrying the very heavy loads of armed conflict.)

Post-Traumatic Stress Disorder

By the time of the Vietnam War, operant conditioning had trained (programmed, if you will) soldiers to "engage" the enemy. The kill ratio was astounding (on the average, twelve enemy soldiers for every one American). Not only had the average American soldier learned how to kill the enemy, he became very good at doing so in unprecedented numbers. But although this new kind of training had taught the soldier how to "switch the safety off," so to speak, it had left him basically unprepared to deal with the emotional and psychological aspects of having killed other human beings. The 90-95 percent fire rate produced by operant conditioning left very little room for posturing. There was, therefore, hardly any way for the average soldier to deny the almost certain fact that he had participated in killing other human beings. Such is—like the resistance to killing that had been overcome by operant conditioning—an equally powerful emotion that, if left unplacated, can cause grave psychological, physiological, and emotional disorders which have conveniently been mish-mashed into a syndrome called Post-Traumatic Stress Disorder (PTSD).

According to the American Psychological Association's *Diagnostic and Statistical Manual of Mental Disorders*, PTSD is described as "a reaction to a psychological traumatic event outside the range of normal experience." The various manifestations of PTSD are many, including recurrent and intrusive dreams and recollections of the experience (called "flashbacks"), emotional blunting, social withdrawal, difficulty or reluctance to initiate or sustain intimate relationships, along with a number of different sleep disturbances. These symptoms, of course, can lead to serious difficulties in readjusting to civilian life, including alcoholism, unemployment, and divorce.

According to the Disabled American Veterans, some 500,000 Vietnam soldiers, Marines, airmen, and sailors suffer from PTSD. The Harris and Associates 1980 estimate was 1.5 million. This means that somewhere between 18 and 54 percent of the 2.8 million military personnel who served in Vietnam have experienced PTSD. Clearly, then, the consequences of asking the military to fight our wars for us takes a tremendous toll on those warriors—a toll the experiences of the Vietnam War and its aftermath only exacerbated.

Studies have shown that the relationship between the degree of intensity of the trauma coupled with the degree of social support received has a direct bearing on the magnitude of the post-traumatic response. Consequently, the Vietnam War, which had a rather wide disapproval rating among Americans, particularly in its latter years, was a virulent breeding ground for PTSD. This is borne out by the following quote:

> Vietnam was an American nightmare that hasn't yet ended for veterans of the war. In the rush to forget the debacle that became our longest war, America found it necessary to conjure up a scapegoat and transferred the heavy burden of blame onto the shoulders of the Vietnam veteran. It's been a crushing weight for them to carry. Rejected by the nation that sent them off to war, the veterans have been plagued with guilt and resentment which has created an identity crises unknown to veterans of previous wars.[15]

A Job Left Largely Undone

During the Vietnam era, millions of American adolescents (for these are the ones who, more than any other, fight our wars) were programmed (or "conditioned") to do something they naturally had a strong disinclination for doing—namely, killing other human beings. But if we believe there are times when it is necessary to fight wars, and who but a hardcore pacifist would think

---

[15] A statement made by D. Andrade and cited by Grossman, p. 282.

otherwise, then it is necessary to teach our soldiers to survive on the battlefield. And to do so, they must learn how to kill, instinctively and efficiently—the more instinctively and the more efficiently, the better. Otherwise, they will, more than likely, face either stalemate or defeat. *But to teach our soldiers how to kill without dealing morally, honestly, intelligently, and forthrightly with the psychological effects of having killed is morally reprehensible.* In other words, the way this country treated our Vietnam veterans was a shame and disgrace. Young men who needed desperately to be commended for the tremendous sacrifice they made for their country and the South Vietnamese, were sorely disparaged and abused, some to the point of even being spat upon when they returned to this country, and all of this shamefully enflamed by the liberal media which were, for the most part, anti-war in their sentiments. What this means is that a morally decadent, self-absorbed, self-indulged American society messed over these young adolescents twice: (1) when we taught them how to be effective killers and sent them to fight a foreign war that our politicians seemed not to have a clue as to what we were doing there in the first place, and (2) by treating these young warriors as pariahs when they were finally permitted to come home.

History Determined To Repeat Itself

I am fearful that as the current rhetoric continues to heat up in the press and the halls of Congress over our troops' continued stay in Iraq, many of those who are in harm's way every day are being discouraged in the difficult and dangerous work they have been sent to do on our behalf, and on the behalf of the Iraqi people. "Chappaquiddick Ted" Kennedy and his anti-war cohorts in Congress, along with two ex-presidents (Bill "I never touched that woman" Clinton and Jimmy "I won the Noble Peace Prize" Carter), with the encouragement, once again, of the liberal (and not so liberal) media, are doing their very best to turn the "War on Terror" being fought in Iraq into a disgraceful sham they are claiming was wrongly conceived and perpetuated by a commander-in-chief who lied and manipulated us into war. Consequently, our warfighters are now being bombarded with the accusations (implied or otherwise) that the war they are fighting (killing and being killed) is not a just war, after all, and that their actions in this war, therefore, are not righteous. Just think of the devastating toll such a constant barrage will have on these men while in theater and when they return home. Will we ever learn?

I certainly do not intend to demean those who fought WW II, the so-called "Greatest Generation." It was a fine one, alright, but really not much different from the kind that came before or after. The thing that made that generation so different than those since, mostly has to do, I think, with the fact that it was the last generation of Americans to have the luxury of fighting a "good war," as WW II is sometimes described. But it was "good" only in that it was a just war fought for the right reason. But how it was, in fact, prosecuted and fought is an entirely different story, as I have tried to point out in an earlier chapter. Nevertheless, those Americans who fought in that war believed their cause was just and this was, no doubt, of some solace to those who found it necessary to kill the enemy, whether German or Japanese. The media and the folks back home were very supportive of what their WW II soldiers, Marines, airmen, and sailors were doing. Finally, when these American war-fighters returned home, they did so to a very warm welcome by a civilian population that had been prepared and helped to understand them through movies like *The Man in the Gray Flannel Suit*, *The Best Years of Our Lives*, and *Pride of the Marines*. This is not to say there were no cases of PTSD (although it wasn't called that back then). There were. But, on the whole, that generation of war-fighters adjusted well and became very productive members of society.

The Vietnam war was quite different. We had not been "attacked," as in WW II, therefore there was no "dastardly deed" that would "live in infamy," a deed that needed to be justly recompensed. Consequently, the war in Vietnam was, from the beginning, problematic. Fighting a war in a far away place to keep "dominos" from falling to the Communists was a hard concept for Americans living in an unprecedented time of peace and prosperity to get a grip on (the "domino theory" was a 20th Century, Cold War foreign policy theory that speculated, and I think correctly so, if one key nation in a region came under the control of

Communists, others would follow one after the other). The American public's lack of comprehension in the middle years of the 1960s no doubt contributed to the unpopularity of a war that would be waged in the jungles, rice paddies, and villages of a seemingly insignificant Third World country in Southeast Asia—a war that would become, before it was over some ten years later, one of the most divisive wars in our nation's history. The veterans who fought in that war would ultimately be depicted in the American media and world press as "depraved fiends" and "psychopathic killers." The beautiful young movie stars of that era (the ones who would become the anti-war loonies of today) led the accusatory chant of a nation that openly called them "baby-killers," "murderers," and "butchers."

Vietnam: A Watershed Moment That Changed Us Forever

In the poignant prologue to their runaway *New York Times* bestseller, *We Were Soldiers Once...And Young*, a book that is undoubtedly the most significant piece of work to come out of the Vietnam War, Lt. Gen. Harold G. "Hal" Moore (Ret.) and Joseph L. Galloway, who at the time the book was published was a senior writer for the *U. S. News & World Report*, captured the watershed moment in late 1965 that was, from a practical point of view, the real beginning of the Vietnam War—a war that would dramatically change us as a nation. In their magnificent prologue on pages xxi-xxv, they wrote:

> This story is about time and memories. The time was 1965, a different kind of year, a watershed year when one era was ending in America and another was beginning. We felt it then, in the many ways our lives changed so suddenly, so dramatically, and looking back on it from a quarter-century gone we are left in no doubt. It was the year America decided to directly intervene in the Byzantine affairs of obscure and distant Vietnam. It was the year we went to war. In the broad, traditional sense, that "we" who went to war was all of us, all Americans, though in truth at that time the larger majority had little knowledge of, less interest in, and no great concern with what was beginning so far away.

So this story is about the smaller, more tightly focused "we" of that sentence: the first American combat troops, who boarded World War II-era troopships, sailed to that little-known place, and fought the first major battle of a conflict that would drag on for ten long years and come as near to destroying America as it did to destroying Vietnam.

...

We were the children of the 1950s and we went where we were sent because we love our country. We were draftees, most of us, but we were proud of the opportunity to serve that country just as our father had served in World War II and our older brothers had in Korea. We were members of an elite, experimental combat division trained in the new art of airmobile warfare at the behest of President John F. Kennedy.

...

We were the children of the 1950s and John F. Kennedy's young stalwarts of the early 1960s. He told the world that we would "pay any price, bear any burden, meet any hardship" in the defense of freedom. We were the down payment on that costly contract, but the man who signed it was not there when we fulfilled his promise. John F. Kennedy waited for us on a hill in Arlington National Cemetery, and in time we came by the thousands to fill those slopes with our white marble markers and to ask on the murmur of the wind if that was truly the future he had envisioned for us.

...

The class of 1965 came out of the old America, a nation that disappeared forever in the smoke that billowed off the jungle battlegrounds where we fought and bled. The country that sent us off to war was not there to welcome us home. It no longer existed. We answered the call of one president who was now dead; we followed the orders of another who would be hounded from office, and haunted, by the war he mismanaged so badly.

...

As the years passed we searched each other out and found that the half-remembered pride of service was shared by those who had shared everything else with us. With them, and only with them, could we talk about what had really happened over there—what we had seen, what we had done, what we had survived.

We knew what Vietnam had been like, and how we looked and acted and talked and smelled. No one in America did. Hollywood got it wrong every...time, whetting twisted political knives on the bones of our dead brothers.

So once, just this once: This is how it all began, what it was really like, what it meant to us, and what we meant to each other. It was no movie. When it was over the dead did not get up and dust themselves off and walk away. The wounded did not wash away the red and go on with life, unhurt. Those who were...unscratched were by no means untouched. Not one of us left Vietnam the same young man he was when he arrived.

After paying tribute to the 234 young Americans who died beside them during four days in November, 1965 at Landing Zone X-Ray and Landing Zone Albany in the Ia Drang Valley, Republic of South Vietnam, and the seventy more of their comrades who died in the skirmishes before and after the big battle, names engraved on the third panel to the right of the apex, Panel 3-East, of the Vietnam Veterans Memorial in Washington, D. C., and on their hearts, Moore and Galloway concluded with the following words:

While those who have never known war may fail to see the logic, this story also stands as a tribute to the hundreds of young men of the 320th, 33rd, and 66th Regiments of the People's Army of Vietnam who died by our hands in that place. They, too, fought and died bravely. They were a worthy enemy. We who killed them pray that their bones were recovered from that wild, desolate place where we left them, and taken home for decent and honorable burial.

This is our story and theirs. For we were soldiers once, and young.

It is a crying shame that the Vietnam veteran was treated so shabbily by his countrymen. It is a disgrace that we did not give these warriors the comfort and understanding they so desperately needed. However, I seriously wonder if America, morally soft and decidedly anti-war in sentiment, as we now are, will ever again be able to fight a protracted war in which there is much death and dying to be done. The Persian Gulf War was short and sweet. There were fewer lives lost in that entire war than were lost in that first major battle of the Vietnam War waged in the Ia Drang Valley of South Vietnam's Central Highlands. Our Persian Gulf War veterans came home to thunderous and glorious celebrations, and that was as it should have been. But many of those same veterans are now grunting it out in Afghanistan and Iraq while being subjected to the constant din of anti-war naysayers and elected public officials who always want to make it "clear" that they are *against* the war but *for* the troops. Hogwash! Anything and everything that can be used to disparage the war is said and done within the electronic earshot of those warriors we have asked to do their duty, killing and being killed. For what? A just cause? No, we were lied into war, we are being told, which is itself a bald-faced lie that continues to be given legs by the media. Even the actions of the few "rotten apples" that have violated the Uniform Code of Military Justice, and are being tried and punished for their misdeeds, are incessantly touted by the media, impugning the character of fine, properly motivated warriors who are trying to do a most difficult job in the most difficult of circumstances in the most difficult of places on the face of the earth.

A New Kind Of Warrior

Ordained by God Himself, soldiering is an honorable, righteous and, therefore, godly profession. In the Old Testament, the Lord, who called Himself a "man of war" or a "warrior," depending on what translation one is using,[16] raised up great warriors who were men of unapologetic faith. Joshua, Gideon, and David are a few who readily come to mind. But there are others, some of whom remain little known to many Bible students, like Shammah, who is mentioned as one of the "mighty men" or "warriors" who David had at his disposal.[17] In 2 Samuel 23:11-12, the following short, but very telling, story is told about the warrior Shammah:

---

[16] See Ex. 15:3.
[17] See 2 Sam. 23:8 and I Chron. 10:10.

And after him was Shammah, the son of Agee the Hararite. The Philistines had gathered together into a troop where there was a piece of ground full of lentils. Then the people fled from the Philistines. But he stationed himself in the middle of the field, defended it, and killed the Philistines. And the Lord brought about a great victory.

Notice that Shammah stood and fought the Philistines after everyone else had run away. Shammah, who was not a "cut-and-run" kind of fellow, "stationed himself in the middle of the field, defended it, and killed the Philistines." One of the principle characteristics of a warrior is that he runs toward, not away from, the action. To those who ran away, that field was just a piece of dirt, a field of lentils. They probably thought such territory wasn't worth that proverbial "hill of beans," and it certainly wasn't worth losing their lives over. So they fled. But not Shammah. Those beans or lentils belonged to God's people, not those "uncircumcised" Philistines, and they were, therefore, worth fighting for, even dying for. Jesus would later say, "He who is faithful in what is least is faithful also in much; and he who is unjust in what is least is unjust also in much."[18]

Therefore, we are not surprised that this man who was willing to defend this field of lentils eventually joined the list of David's mighty men of valor. After all, it was the principle of the thing, wasn't it? Justice and righteousness demanded that Shammah step forward to resist the invaders, even if it cost him his life. I say this because every warrior knows that in order to effectively fight and kill the enemy, he must be willing, if necessary, to shed his own blood. So, we can be sure that when the great warrior Shammah positioned himself in that field that day, he was ready to die, if necessary, for that which he believed to be right and honorable. (Incidentally, no just warrior can be deprived of these and survive. For if he happens to survive physically, his soul has been spiritually, emotionally, even mortally, wounded.) Shammah did so

---

[18] Lk. 16:10.

believing that the God who he served would aid him in his noble task; and He did.

I don't know how many Philistines there were in that "troop," but it wasn't just a few, for the Scriptures tell us that "the Lord brought about a great victory" that day, and for it to be described this way, there can be little doubt that Shammah was greatly outnumbered by the Philistines. But with God's help, he was victorious.

There are many other examples I could cite, but this account serves to demonstrate the point I wish to make at this time, which is this: *if our country could consistently produce and nurture this kind of warrior, it would never have to fear defeat in the "bean fields" of conflict.* Such men would be nurtured as men of valor and honored for their valuable service. They would be the kind of men who believed that death is to be preferred before dishonor. In turn, such gallant warriors would carefully be used in only those skirmishes and wars undertaken to set aright injustice and unrighteousness—skirmishes and wars in which these men would, themselves, always strive to be just. Under these circumstances, American war-fighters would never again have to experience the PTSD bane that infects so many of our modern warriors. Never again would such "mighty men" of valor and war be demeaned by those they sacrificially serve and protect. Never again would our elected officials sharpen their political knives on the bones of those who have bled and died for them. Never again. Never again!

But alas, for this to happen we would need to be a different nation than the one we have become. An affluent, self-absorbed nation that has, for all practical secular purposes, rejected God does not have the insight nor inclination to honor their mighty men of war. The self-righteous, "Thou shall not kill," religionists, who have taken a Biblical concept that prohibits murder and turned it into a condemnation of all wars, as well as the warriors who fight them, have conditioned many soldiers to think of their profession, along with that of their law-enforcement cohorts, as a "dirty-hands" job that must be performed by sinners or, at best, those who are considered to be, ahem, "less spiritual." Consequently, instead of viewing themselves and their work as right and just, post-WW II American soldiers all too frequently are compelled to think of themselves as cold-blooded killers and murderers, and all this inspired by religionists, the media, and the many citizens who have imbibed an anti-war sentiment that says, "There are, perhaps, some things worth dying for, but there is absolutely nothing worth killing for."

The soldiers of such a society will be largely unappreciated as the truly positive force for good they are in a fallen world plagued by sin, strife, and inhumanity. They will be viewed, instead, as a necessary evil that must be kept around to do truly dark and dirty things so the rest of us can live in some sort of relative peace. It is no wonder, then, that the soldiers of such a society suffer the PTSD effects of having killed the enemy, even when doing so was clearly righteous and just. This was, and continues to be, the obvious experience of the Vietnam War veterans, and before it is all over, it will, I fear, be the experience of our Iraq War veterans as well. "God forbid!," we might all collectively say. But "God forbid!" is a rather strange thing for a nation without God to exclaim, is it not?

Chapter 7

The Warrior's Burden (Part 2): A Nation Without God

It has taken us a long time to get to this point as a nation. The "War is Hell" crowd, a rather influential group who viewed war—any war—as a "necessary evil" and was, therefore, willing to use "any means" to end one (after all, "war itself is the enemy, isn't it?"), grew up with and festered in the public square of America alongside of the blight of a sweeping secularization that was not squimish to ask, "What's God got to do with it, anyway?" These two philosophical epidemics were perfect hosts for each other and became a mighty pandemic that changed forever the way many Americans would view all wars and the soldiers who fought them. To such, WW II was a relatively "good war" only in the sense that it was a "necessary evil"—necessary, because the only alternative to such an evil was total capitulation to an even "greater evil," namely fascism, along with its dictators and tyrants. Such thinking about war became the breeding ground for the "Make love, not war" pacifism and social revolution of the 1960s and 70s.

This is why Moore and Galloway, who we talked about in the previous chapter, wrote of 1965 being "a different kind of year, a watershed year when one era was ending in America and another was beginning."[1] They went on to say, you recall, that...

---

[1] Moore, p. xxi.

The class of 1965 came out of the old America, a nation that disappeared forever in the smoke that billowed off the jungle battlegrounds where we fought and bled. The country that sent us off to war was not there to welcome us home. It no longer existed.[2]

It was about this time that state-sanctioned prayer in the public schools of America was deemed by the United States Supreme Court to be "unconstitutional."[3] The atheists and secularists *et al.* have continued to argue that this played no part in the rise of the moral chaos and crime that followed. In their response to the resulting outcry in some sectors of American society, an outcry that cites the subsequent rise of the multitude of problems that have arisen in the public schools of America, the *American Atheists* argue:

We CAN do something about problems in schools, but mandatory or "student led" prayer which violates the rights of students is not the answer. Prayer is being promoted as a "feel good" quickie-fix to complex problems. Madalyn Murray [O'Hair] did indeed help to end prayer recitation in schools; but that did not cause the problems which exist today. Society has changed, and schools must change as well. The answer to problems might well involve doing other things—emphasize science and math to prepare kids for the next century, smaller class sizes, perhaps even better pay for over-worked teachers. Often, these programs cost money and take time. They are not the "instant solution" which the prayer-in-school boosters offer, but they are more substantive.[4]

However, I "thinketh [these atheists] protesteth too much." Obviously, taking prayer out of the public schools of America did not create all the problems that currently exist. And yes, the atheists are right, society *has* changed, but "Why has it changed?"

---

[2] Moore, p. xxiii.

[3] *Engel v. Vitale,* 1962 and *Abington Township School District v. Schempp,* 1963.

[4] View at www.atheists.org/publicschools/faqs.prayer.html#nation.

seems to be a good question. This, however, is the question the secularists and atheists want to ignore. Society has changed because the philosophies these folks imbibe and have evangelistically proclaimed throughout the years have been victorious not just in the marketplace of ideas, but especially in the liberal mindsets of too many of the judges and justices who adjudicate America's courts. Therefore, it cannot be denied that the defeat of state-sponsored prayer in the public schools was an important standard for the secularists to have captured, and no matter what they say, they display it proudly.

Add to this the very visible decline of morality that has been taking place in American culture since the early 1900s, and one realizes why Moore's and Galloway's "Class of 1965" believed they came home to a very different country than the one that sent them to fight in that faraway war. They did! The transition from a *biblical-based morality* that had prevailed in this country up to the early 1900s had, by the time of the start of the Vietnam War, given way to an *abiblical morality* (1900-1950s) that said, "Certain things are right and wrong, but I don't know why," which then gave way to an *immorality* (1960s-early 1970s) that said, "Certain things are right and wrong, but I don't care." However, since the late 1970s, the most viable "morality" in America has simply been *amorality*, or no morality at all—a kind of moral philosophy that rather testily, and haughtily, proclaims, "There is absolutely no such thing as right or wrong!"[5]

So, it was to a country defined by the greed and immorality of the 1970s to which the Class of 1965 returned. It was a country in "malaise," as President Jimmy Carter is supposed to have called it. In fact, Mr. Carter—who was evidently a very honest man but an absolutely pathetic president—never mentioned the word "malaise" in his July 15, 1979 "Crisis of Confidence" speech to the American people. However, in the memo to Carter that prodded the speech, Carter's pollster, Patrick Caddell, had mentioned the

---

[5] See this decline in chart form on my website at http://allanturner.com/chart.html.

word "malaise." Consequently, the speech Carter made that July evening late in his presidency, a speech that—as I'll point out in a moment, certainly got something right—became known, notoriously, as Carter's "Malaise Speech."

In Caddell's original memo to Carter, he says he argued that after fifteen years filled with assassinations, Vietnam, Watergate, and a declining economy (to which can be added gas lines, inflation, recession, the Iran hostage crisis, and an ineffectual and fractured administration), Americans were suffering from a general "crisis of confidence." Address this fundamental problem, he told the president, inspire the country to overcome it, and he would turn his presidency around.

But Carter's speech backfired, big time, and a little more than a year later, Ronald Reagan defeated Carter by selling a substantial portion of the American voters a vision of America that was as optimistic as Carter's had been pessimistic. As historian Douglas Brinkley noted:

[I]t boomeranged on him. The op-ed pieces started spinning out, "Why don't you fix something? There's nothing wrong with the American people. We're a great people. Maybe the problem's in the White House, maybe we need new leadership to guide us."[6]

Historian Roger Wilkins concurred:

When your leadership is demonstrably weaker than it should be, you don't then point at the people and say, "It's your problem." If you want the people to move, you move them the way Roosevelt moved them, or you exhort them the way Kennedy or Johnson exhorted them. You don't say, "It's your fault."[7]

---

[6] The PBS *American Experience* documentary "Jimmy Carter," Adriana Bosch, director, Margaret Drain, executive producer, WGBH Educational Foundation, 2002.

[7] *Ibid.*

But whether the American people agreed with him or not, the peanut farmer from Plains, Georgia had gotten some things right in that sermon—oops, I mean, speech. Much of it was, in fact, amazingly right, and I referred to it as a "sermon" because that's what a good portion of it was—a sermon to an amoral America that had lost its biblical faith. In fact, Hendrik Hertzberg, who worked on the malaise speech, actually admits that it...

> was more like a sermon than a political speech. It had the themes of confession, redemption, and sacrifice. He was bringing the American people into this spiritual process that he had been through, and presenting them with an opportunity for redemption as well as redeeming himself.[8]

In the speech, Mr. Carter admonished the American people by saying:

> In a nation that was proud of hard work, strong families, close-knit communities and our faith in God, too many of us now tend to worship self-indulgence and consumption. Human identity is no longer defined by what one does but by what one owns. But we've discovered that owning things and consuming things does not satisfy our longing for meaning. We've learned that piling up material goods cannot fill the emptiness of lives which have no confidence or purpose.

In another place, he said:

> First of all, we must face the truth, and then we can change our course. We simply must have faith in each other, faith in our ability to govern ourselves, and faith in the future of this nation. Restoring that faith and that confidence to America is now the most important task we face. It is a true challenge of this generation of Americans.

---

[8] *Ibid.*

Preach on, Mr. Carter:

> The threat is nearly invisible in ordinary ways. It is a crisis of confidence. It is a crisis that strikes at the very heart and soul and spirit of our national will. We can see this crisis in the growing doubt about the meaning of our own lives and in the loss of a unity of purpose for our nation.
>
> The erosion of our confidence in the future is threatening to destroy the social and the political fabric of America.
>
> The confidence that we have always had as a people is not simply some romantic dream or a proverb in a dusty book that we read just on the Fourth of July.
>
> It is the idea which founded our nation and has guided our development as a people. Confidence in the future has supported everything else — public institutions and private enterprise, our own families, and the very Constitution of the United States. Confidence has defined our course and has served as a link between generations. We've always believed in something called progress. We've always had a faith that the days of our children would be better than our own.
>
> Our people are losing that faith, not only in government itself but in the ability as citizens to serve as the ultimate rulers and shapers of our democracy. As a people we know our past and we are proud of it. Our progress has been part of the living history of America, even the world. We always believed that we were part of a great movement of humanity itself called democracy, involved in the search for freedom, and that belief has always strengthened us in our purpose. But just as we are losing our confidence in the future, we are also beginning to close the door on our past.

He concluded by saying:

> In closing, let me say this: I will do my best, but I will not do it alone. Let your voice be heard. Whenever you have a chance, say something good about our country. With God's help and for the sake of our Nation, it is time for us to join hands in America. Let us commit ourselves together to a rebirth of the American spirit. Working together with our common faith we cannot fail.

But the America to which Mr. Carter spoke that July evening in 1979 had already lost its religion, and with it the moral base that would oblige its citizens to rally to his call.

So, having lost their religion and inundated with the anti-war, pacifist philosophies that have caught hold in modern America, many Americans have come to view war as simply unpalatable. For many others, "imperial America" is thought to be *the* locus of evil in the world. Consequently, many Americans do not view their soldiers as good men actively engaged in the doing of justice and righteousness. Instead, they view them as depraved killers and misfits who deserve the PTSD that so frequently plagues them. So evil is the military and those who serve it perceived to be by many in our society, there are even high schools and colleges in this nation that prohibit military recruiters from coming on their campuses.

The New Centurion

This is a far cry from the favorable light in which the New Testament Scriptures depict several Roman military officers. The first of these is a centurion (a company commander) stationed in Capernaum who asked Jesus to heal one of his servants who was gravely ill.[9] As a centurion, this man served as the backbone of the Roman army. What we learn from this account about his superb character jibes with the historical repute in which Roman centurions were generally held. Polybius described ideal centurions as...

> possessing the faculty for command, steady and serious; not prone to rush into battle nor eager to strike the first blow, but ready to die in defense of their posts if their men are overborne by number and hard pressed.[10]

---

[9] See Matt. 8:5-13; Luke 7:1-10.
[10] *A Dictionary of Christ and the Gospels*, I, p. 276.

Even so, concern for a slave was a rare thing in Roman society. But according to Luke, this man's servant "was dear to him." This demonstrates the genuine tenderness of this warrior leader—a man, no doubt, made up of both steel and velvet.

Furthermore, the centurion's reverence of an itinerant Jewish preacher was highly unusual for the culture of which he was a part. Instead of using his position to command Jesus to heal his servant, he simply pleaded with Him to do so. Calling Him "Lord," the centurion acknowledged Jesus' superior authority, humbly exclaiming that he was not even worthy that Jesus should come under his roof. Using the authority he had as a military officer to command others to do what he said as an example, the centurion acknowledged that all Jesus would have to do is speak the word and his servant would be healed.

When Jesus heard the centurion's profession, "He marveled," Matthew 8:10 records, "and said to those who followed, 'Assuredly, I say to you, I have not found such great faith, not even in Israel!'" What a wonderful tribute the Lord paid to the faith of this Roman soldier with those words. No greater faith, He said, not even in Israel. Wow! If the United States of America could produce and honor such men today, it would have nothing to fear from its enemies, for God has always rewarded such valor and faith with great victories. But there is more.

In Acts 10:1-48, the reader of the New Testament hears of the conversion of Cornelius, one of at least six centurions who made up the cohort of hoplites[11] in Caesarea known as the "Italian Regiment." These were not conscripts, as was frequently the case, but were loyal Romans from Italy. As Caesarea was the most prominent city in Palestine at the time, functioning as the virtual capital, it was the usual home of the Roman governor of Judea. Consequently, it is even possible that the Italian Regiment served the province not just as the keepers of the peace, but as the governor's special bodyguard as well. They were, and here's my point,

---

[11] Somewhere between 600 to 1000 foot soldiers.

the best Rome had to offer and Cornelius was one of their magnificent leaders.

Consequently, it is most interesting to hear how Luke described Cornelius in verse 2. He was, he said, "a devout man and one who feared God with all his household, who gave alms generously to the people, and prayed to God always." Anyone, particularly a religious teacher, who doesn't think a soldier can be a fierce warrior and a devoutly spiritual man all at the same time just doesn't know his Bible. The Bible is simply replete with stories of devoutly spiritual men who were ferociously effective warriors. To kill, when justice and righteousness demand it, is not a sin. To rescue the helpless at the hands of the merciless and cold-blooded, even when such requires the rescuer to inflict serious bodily harm or even death, is not a sin so long as the rescuer acts consistent with the principles of justice and righteousness set forth in the Bible. And to risk one's life in order to serve and protect one's fellowman is neither suicidal nor idiotic. It is, instead, a noble exhibition of what true sacrificial love is all about. Cornelius, the Roman soldier par excellence, surely became Cornelius, the Christian soldier par excellence, and it is this man and his devotion to God that serves as the model for what I am calling "the new centurion."

An army, air force, navy or Marine Corp made up of new centurions would be a formidable force for good. They would serve and protect their countrymen honorably and faithfully, never using their various strengths and abilities to intimidate, oppress or take advantage of those they are sworn to protect.[12] They would be strong and courageous, but never ruffians or bullies. Although they would be the fiercest and mightiest of warriors, they would never murder, rape or pillage. Although they would be effective and efficient in the various tasks of killing their enemies, they would always treat them fairly and honorably, rejecting atrocity in any form.

On the new centurion's watch, there would be nothing unsavory or unwholesome to report—no My Lias nor Abu Ghraibs. For

---

[12] See Lk. 3:14.

sure, there would be death and dying, for such is the nature of war. For certain, the anti-war media would always depict such death and dying in the worse light possible. Yes, totally innocent non-combatants will always die in war (it's called, as was previously pointed out, "collateral damage"), but the new centurion would never intentionally target civilians. In fact, he would rather die than do so, for he lives with the enduring ethos that teaches "Death before dishonor" is not just some proverbial military slogan, but is, instead, the difficult, but right, choice of all true warriors.[13] It was Daniel Webster who said:

> If we work on marble, it will perish; if on brass, time will efface it; if we rear up temples, they will crumble into dust; but if we work upon immortal minds and imbue them with principles, with the just fear of God and the love of our fellow men, we engrave on those tablets something that will brighten to all eternity.

Thus, on the mind and in the heart of every true warrior is the desire to do only that which is right, or to honorably die trying. This, then, is the epithet of the humble soldier. It is the embodiment of every true warrior. It is the story of those who were, are, and will be faithful to their God in all things. It is the story of the new centurion.

But until, and unless, America repents towards God, there will be but a pitiful handful of these new centurions to serve as the leaven that could, if given the chance, leaven the "whole lump."[14] Unless America truly repents, it will continue to view the military as an overcompensated bunch of rowdies who must be kept on the payroll so they can do their dark and dirty work when the need arises—a "necessary evil," and all that jazz. Under such circumstances, many soldiers will attempt to live up to (or maybe I should say, down to) the bad-boy image projected onto their profession, cussing, drinking, and whoring their way to the difficult

---

[13] See I Thess. 5:22.
[14] See Matt 13:33.

and largely thankless tasks they are regularly asked to perform around the world.

However, a fighting force of new centurions would eventually quell and largely put an end to such ungodly, foolish, and completely unmanly behavior. Instead of soldiers thinking it manly to take the name of the Lord their God in vain, continually dulling their moral senses with strong drink and loose women, they would reverence their Creator through the right and commendable things they conscientiously say and do as brave and courageous cohorts in the honorable profession of soldiering. The new centurions would never be coarse nor crass. Instead, they would be pure and just in all their actions. And above all, they would be both intelligent and wise.

Intelligent And Wise: Necessary Characteristics Of The Just Warrior

Maybe you didn't like it when I said America has lost its religion and needs to repent and that this is all somehow related to our military effectiveness. After all, isn't America simply the mightiest nation on the planet earth, the big dog on the block, if you will? Yes, it is. Well, isn't it simply unsurpassed in military might, then? Yes, it is. So, isn't it, therefore, unbeatable? No, it isn't. America can, and will, be defeated if it continues down that slippery slope of moral decay it is presently traveling. The Almighty God, the One who rules the nations with a rod of iron[15] has taken down many of the mightiest nations that ever existed on the face of the earth. Babylon and Rome are but two examples. "Righteousness exalts a nation," He has repeatedly told us, "but sin is a reproach [i.e., a "shame" and "disgrace"] to any people."[16]

As sad as it is, it simply cannot be denied that America has lost its way morally. It has summarily rejected that absolute standard of Righteousness taught in the Bible—a standard that is

---

[15] See Psa. 2:9; Rev. 2:27.
[16] Prov. 14:34.

necessary if acts of Justice are to be consistently carried out. Consequently, without national repentance, everything that was once thought to be morally right in our country will be questioned and ultimately rejected. And without such repentance, Divine judgment will surely come.[17] The Bible makes it very clear that God's adversaries, when the time is right, will meet the fire of His wrath.[18] Why? Because they have seen fit to neglect His absolute standard of Righteousness.[19] Again, the only hope we have of escaping this judgment is national repentance.

Fortunately, the new centurions, like the men of Issachar who were mentioned along with David's mighty men of war,[20] will be gallant warriors who will have an understanding of the times in which they live and will, therefore, know what America "ought to do."[21] They will, then, be beacons to a people who have morally lost their way. They will be the salt that savors the decaying ethical infrastructure of this once great nation. As wise men, they will understand their culture and the forces at work behind the scenes, and they will know the path America should take. But like those wise chieftains of Issachar, who were only two hundred out of the tens of thousands who David had at his disposal, the new centurions will, at first, be only a few. But these few could easily be the answer to a prayer that was penned by Dr. Josiah Gilbert Holland way back in the 19th century, a prayer I have frequently appropriated for use in my own private devotions, and one that is easily transferable to the kind of warriors I've been describing. He said:

> God give us men. A time like this demands strong minds, great hearts, true faith, and ready hands; men whom the lust of office cannot buy; men who will not lie; men who will stand before a demagogue and damn his treacherous flatteries without winking; tall men,

---

[17] See Isa. 13-23; Jer. 46-51; Ezek. 25-32; Amos 1-2, *et cetera*.
[18] See Gen. 15:16.
[19] See Psa. 97:1-9.
[20] See I Chron. 12.
[21] See v. 32.

sun-crowned, who live above the fog in public duty and private thinking.

Dr. Holland was, no doubt, thinking of political leaders, but the characteristics and attributes he described are those that should be possessed by every man, particularly the warrior, and the new centurion does. All of David's mighty men of war were surely men of valor, but only the two hundred chieftains of Issachar had the discernment to know what Israel really needed to do at that critical moment in their history. In other words, they were wise men who knew what needed to be done, namely, that David, God's anointed, needed to be placed on the throne of Israel. Likewise, a handful of men (the new centurions) know that God, once again, needs to be enthroned in the collective mind of Americans. It is then, and only then, that the few will become the many, forming an army, navy, air force, and Marine Corp of men who will reflect the spirit of the new centurions, a happy band of brothers who will willingly and virtuously shed their blood for a righteous and just cause.

As men of wisdom, the new centurions will appreciate that discernment (that is, knowing) is "better than weapons of war" (Eccl. 9:18). Such men, exhibiting the characteristics mentioned by Polybius in his description of the Roman centurion, will not be "prone to rush into battle nor eager to strike the first blow." In other words, the new centurions are not brawlers, itching for a fight or war. They know, often intimately, the cost of violence and the high fee it exacts from those who participate in it. Therefore, the pure warrior, contrary to popular thinking, is never the first to call for war, for he knows war's terrible toll. But more importantly, the wise warrior understands that in order for a war to be considered just, it must always be the last resort. This does not rule out a preemptive strike, as many suppose, but it does argue that the latter would only be justified after all reasonable efforts have been made to resolve the matter through other means.

Rejecting, as they must, the quick resort to war, the new centurions know that their ultimate purpose is to be ready, when necessary, to fight and win wars. They will, therefore, while praying for peace, keep themselves fit and ready for battle. In Proverbs 24:5-6, the Scriptures say,

> A wise man is strong, yes, a man of knowledge increases his strength; for by wise counsel you will wage your own war, and in a multitude of counselors there is safety.

So, the old adage that says, "Pray for peace, but prepare for war," is indeed a Biblical concept, and the one who faithfully does that is never a warmonger who sees war as the quick solution to thorny problems.

Those who thought the Civil War would be a quick one were terribly mistaken. Those who thought our troubles in Iraq would be quickly dispatched were wrong. Those who think wars can be "short and sweet" are not wise, nor are they well versed in history. In truth, wars are usually protracted events that are *always* bitter and *never* sweet, and the new centurions, who are as wise as they are strong, know it.

The Toll Of Taking Human Life

As we have learned in this study, the toll the warrior pays for having taken human life is tremendous. Man, who is innately resistant to taking another human being's life, cannot kill his fellowman without experiencing strong emotional and psychological trauma. Contrary to the thinking of many, and I speak especially to religionists, man is not born a callous lowlife who cannot keep from sinning. Man is a free moral agent who often innately knows what is right and wrong.[22] Man's problem is not that he cannot keep from sinning, inherently lacking the ability to resist temptation. In other words, his problem is not that he can't keep from sinning, but that having the free moral agency to resist sinning, he goes ahead and sins anyway. This, then, is man's plight: he is a sinner. Consequently, when man is wrongly conditioned,

---

[22] See Rom. 2:14-15.

religiously or otherwise, to think all killing is somehow sinful, and then he is programmed to kill, as the modern American soldier is, it is reasonable that he will suffer intense guilt at having killed in combat, even when he thinks such killing was necessary. Enter, then, PTSD, the curse of modern soldiers in the West.

All Killing Isn't Murder, Therefore All Killing Isn't Wrong

Grossman, who I mentioned earlier and who is a psychologist, mentions several of the techniques he uses to help soldiers suffering from PTSD. One is to encourage his patients to confront their use of the word "murder." When he can get these patients to see that what they did was in self-defense, and if it occurred in the street tomorrow no charges would be filed, they frequently exclaim, "I never looked at it that way." Grossman goes on to say that this is a common and repeated theme in such counseling.[23]

Another technique is to discuss with his patients what the Bible actually says about killing that is done consistent with justice and righteousness. He discusses with these patients what some of those circumstances might be, including the specific events the patients were involved in. Realizing there is a body of belief in America that thinks it is not "good" to be a soldier, and that much of this is founded on a misunderstanding of the commandment "Thou shalt not kill," Grossman points out that within the "realm of Christianity" there is great disagreement on this matter, and that it is not nearly as simple as some want to make it. So, for the sake of therapy among soldiers, Grossman has discovered there is great value in presenting the other side of the theological debate about killing.[24]

As I've pointed out frequently in this study, there is nothing wrong with soldiering or killing, as long as these are done consistent with the justice and righteousness articulated in the Bible. The new centurion knows this. Consequently, he does not view

---

[23] Grossman, p. 337.
[24] I thank God for Grossman's courage and insight, for such is rare in his overwhelmingly secularized profession.

himself as engaged in something that is unjust and, therefore, ungodly. Instead, he rightly discerns that soldiering, if done consistent with justice and righteousness, is an honorable profession, and that killing in the circumstances of war is sometimes necessary, but never joyous. To take another human being's life—a fellow creature who is made in God's image—will always be unpleasant and even regrettable. But, and here is my point, when it is done righteously, it is never something that needs to be repented of. This, I believe, will serve as a major factor in avoiding the PTSD that plagues the modern American soldier.

Paying The "War Is Hell" Piper

This means that those in our past who believed war-fighting, by its very nature, must take place in a moral vacuum, were wrong. As a result, our soldiers have been paying the terrible price for such wrong-headedness ever since. For if all wars are immoral, and this is what too many Americans now think, then there can be no moral warriors, no new centurions. If all war is hell, as Gen. Sherman argued, then there can be no heavenly hope for those who engage in it. Consequently, PTSD is a terrible curse that accompanies a wrong way of thinking about war, in general, and those who do the fighting, in particular. Thus, it is Sherman and those who bought into his immoral doctrine, and not war itself, who are the real villains here. Under the tutelage of such thinking, soldiers who have done those things they believed duty required of them, even though they thought such things were clearly immoral, have paid dearly, physically, psychologically, and spiritually. And it is precisely these pathogens that make up what we're talking about when referring to PTSD. For to take human life in war while doubting the righteousness of one's cause, or while questioning the means being used to prosecute a war, is a PTSD accident waiting to happen. Modern America has sown the wind in this regard and is now reaping the whirlwind.[25] The idea that one must do ugly, dishonorable things in order to prevent even uglier and more morally reprehensible things from happening finds justification in the pragmatism of the humanistic thinking that has been busy sweeping away the Biblical foundation for morality that once ruled this country. As they say where I come from, "The chickens have come home to roost," and in the overall murkiness and morass of such an immoral and amoral universe, soldiers frequently do not know whether their cause is just or their killing righteous. What a pathetic situation. What a disastrous result. What a shame and disgrace. Only evil men should feel such guilt. Only sinners should experience such things and carry such doubts; not the good and honorable soldier who fights to "deliver those who are drawn toward death, and hold[s] back those stumbling to the slaughter."[26] Surely this ought not to be the plight of those who have "broke[n] the fangs of the wicked and plucked the victim from his teeth,"[27] for the God who is the Creator and Sustainer of the universe, the One who has Himself "broken the teeth of the ungodly,"[28] would not heap such burdens on the righteous deeds of those who walk uprightly in war.

No, no, no! The God of heaven does not condemn the warrior (be he policeman or soldier) who is acting godly, and neither should those who call themselves Christians. To justly fight a just war is not inherently sinful. It is, in fact, the very opposite. For to do justly, to love mercy, and to walk humbly (i.e., by faith) with God, as is pointed out in Micah 6:8, is, we are told in Ecclesiastes 12:13, "the whole duty of man." I've said it several times already, but I'm going to say it one more time: *It breaks my heart that we have come to treat our soldiers so shabbily.* When America renews its collective faith in the Creator and the Holy Scriptures He has provided us, soldiers acting righteously will be honored as true

---

[25] See Hos. 8:7.
[26] Prov. 24:11.
[27] Job 29:17.
[28] Psa. 3:7.

"servants of God"[29] and as the valuable members of society they really are.

Already At Work

But by speaking of these new centurions mostly in the future tense, I do not mean to imply that there are not now new centurions who ply their difficult and emotionally taxing trade with the utmost integrity. As always, there are. They know *who* and *what* they are, and they know *why* they are different. But they are the few, not the many. Given the chance, they will be "force multipliers," to use a military term, that will, in turn, nurture and mentor others to be like themselves. Together these will be a redoubtable force for good in our dangerous and increasingly hostile world. When this country of ours gets back to its core values, these men, these new centurions, will be honored, respected, and yes, even feared; for Romans 13:3-4 says:

> Do you want to be unafraid of the authority? Do what is good, and you will have praise from the same. For he is God's minister to you for good. But if you do evil, be afraid; for he does not bear the sword in vain; for he is God's minister, an avenger to execute wrath on him who practices evil.

I fervently pray and look forward to the dawning of such a day in the America I greatly love, even with its moral flaws and general irreligiosity. After all, this is the America that others have bled and died for so that I (and others) could continue to enjoy the freedoms this country provides. Furthermore, and more importantly, it is the America my son and daughter and their children will live in after I have gone home to be with the Lord. I would love for it to be a rejuvenated America where God is worshipped and just warriors are rightly honored. I would love for it to be a nation where its angst-ridden citizens would know the

---

[29] Rom. 13:1-7.

forgiveness of their sins through a relationship with the precious blood of Jesus Christ.

May it be so, Lord...may it be so.

Chapter 8

What About Nuclear Weapons?

On Sunday morning, August 6, 1945, the cross hairs on the bombsight of the Enola Gay, an American B-29 Superfortress, was fixed on the Aioic Bridge in the Japanese city of Hiroshima. Within minutes of the dropping of "Little Boy," the nickname of the first atomic bomb used on a metropolitan center, Hiroshima lay in ashes. Of its 343,969 civilian residents, 78,150 were killed. Another 37,425 were wounded and 13,000 were missing.

More than a decade later on the T.V. program, "This is Your Life," Mr. Kiyoshi Tanimoto, a Methodist minister in Hiroshima on that fateful day, met face to face with the copilot of the Enola Gay, Robert A. Lewis. Both men were asked to relate the first thoughts that raced through their minds after the blast. Mr. Tanimoto said he fell to the ground saying, "Oh God, what has happened?" Capt. Lewis, after circling the city and observing the pillar of smoke, said he'd thought, "My God, what have we done?" This is reflected in his journal, which says:

> Fifteen seconds after the flash there were two very distinct slaps and that was all the physical effects we felt. We turned the ship so we could observe results and there in front of our eyes was without a doubt the greatest explosion man had ever witnessed. The city was 9/10 covered with smoke and a column of white cloud, which in less than three minutes reached 30,000 feet and then went up to 50,000 feet. I honestly have the feeling of groping for words to explain this or I might say, my God, what have we done? Everyone on the ship is actually dumbstruck, even though we had expected something fierce.

Today, at the beginning of a new millennium, Mr. Tanimoto's and Capt. Lewis' questions continue to be appropriate when thinking about nuclear weapons.

As I've tried to make clear in this study, it is not possible for me, as an advocate of "Just War" doctrine, to morally justify President Truman's decision to drop atomic bombs on the Japanese cities of Hiroshima and Nagasaki. To argue, as he did afterwards, that the decision ultimately saved untold American and Japanese lives is of no value to me as a moral argument. Yes, there is the very real possibility that the President's decision did save many more lives than it took, and this remains one of the major reasons given by those who defend it. But that a particular action is pragmatic and utilitarian does not a morally satisfying biblical argument make.

Yes, there was every reason to believe Mr. Truman's decision saved American lives. It was believed by some that the war with Japan, which still had an estimated two million plus soldiers available for fighting in defense of the homeland, could continue late into 1946. In fact, that an all-out invasion of Japan would have resulted in a furiously resisted, last-ditch effort on the part of the Japanese to defend their island had been amply evidenced by the Battle of Okinawa, which took place in April, May and June of 1945. In that battle the Americans experienced almost 80,000 casualties, the Japanese garrison experienced more than 90,000 men killed in action (only 10,600 prisoners were taken), and worst of all, the Okinawans lost more than 100,000 people, the vast majority of whom were civilians. All this being true, many facts remain unknown to most Americans. The following article, I think, provides a much better understanding of the events of that time:

Almost six decades after the fact, the 1945 unleashing of an atomic bomb on Hiroshima continues to be the subject of impassioned debate. Every year the bombing anniversary— which falls on August 6—occasions heated exchanges between those who question the atomic bombing and those who adamantly defend President Harry Truman's use of the weapon on Japanese cities. In this debate Truman's most fervent defenders are World War II veterans and their self-appointed champions in the media.

Most Americans have heard World War II veterans claim that the atomic destruction of Hiroshima and Nagasaki saved their lives. This historical argument often leads to another: that those who fought against the Japanese, or who expected to be part of an invasion of Japan, are of one mind in believing that the use of the atomic bomb was unquestionably the right decision at the time.

Relayed through family stories, media portraits and political soundbites, this "you weren't there and therefore don't have any right to offer your views" argument discourages thoughtful discussion of one of the most important decisions in American history. And it contradicts the more informed opinion of some of the top officers these veterans served under.

Indeed, contrary to conventional opinion today, many military leaders of the time—including six out of seven five-star officers—criticized the use of the atomic bomb.

Take, for example, Admiral William Leahy, White House chief of staff and chairman of the Joint Chiefs of Staff during the war. Leahy wrote in his 1950 memoirs that "the use of this barbarous weapon at Hiroshima and Nagasaki was of no material assistance in our war against Japan. The Japanese were already defeated and ready to surrender." Moreover, Leahy continued, "in being the first to use it, we had adopted an ethical standard common to the barbarians of the Dark Ages. I was not taught to make war in that fashion, and wars cannot be won by destroying women and children."

President Dwight Eisenhower, the Allied commander in Europe during World War II, recalled in 1963, as he did on several other occasions, that he had opposed using the atomic bomb on Japan during a July 1945 meeting with Secretary of War Henry Stimson: "I told him I was against it on two counts. First, the Japanese were ready to surrender and it wasn't necessary to hit them with that awful thing. Second, I hated to see our country be the first to use such a weapon."

Admiral William "Bull" Halsey, the tough and outspoken commander of the U.S. Third Fleet, which participated in the American offensive against the Japanese home islands in the final months of the war, publicly stated in 1946 that "the first atomic bomb was an unnecessary experiment." The Japanese, he noted, had "put out a lot of peace feelers through Russia long before" the bomb was used.

Lacking the knowledge of these and other military leaders, rank-and-file veterans tend to support the bomb's use. Contrary to popular belief, however, not all Pacific war veterans applaud the atomic annihilation of two Japanese cities.

Responding to a journalist's question in 1995 about what he would have done had he been in Truman's shoes, Joseph O'Donnell, a retired marine corps sergeant who served in the Pacific, answered that "we should have went [sic] after the military in Japan. They were bad. But to drop a bomb on women and children and the elderly, I draw a line there, and I still hold it."

Doug Dowd, a Pacific-theater rescue pilot who was slated to take an early part in the invasion of Japan if it had come to that, recently stated that it was clear in the final months of the war that the Japanese "had lost the ability to defend themselves." American planes "met little, and then virtually no resistance," Dowd recalled. He added, "It is well-known [now] that the Japanese were seeking to make a peace agreement well before Hiroshima."

Or take Ed Everts, a major in the 7th weather squadron of the Army Air Corps. Everts, who received an air medal for surviving a crash at sea during the battle at Iwo Jima, told us that America's use of atomic bombs was "a war crime" for which "our leaders should have been put on trial as were the German and Japanese leaders."

While the great sacrifice and heroism of veterans should never be forgotten, their often impassioned defense of the bombing of Hiroshima does us all a disservice. It substitutes a simplistic history for a complex set of events. It narrows historical evidence about a White House decision to the question of what soldiers in the Pacific believed, when the relevant historical question is what decisionmakers thought at the time.

It allows us to forget, or easily marginalize, those brave and patriotic men—such as Admiral Leahy and Sergeant O'Donnell—who have questioned President Truman's fateful decision.

Last, it creates a fog of patriotic orthodoxy that makes it hard for Americans to have an honest debate and disagreement about this contentious issue. Criticism of the atomic bomb should not be interpreted as disrespect for World War II veterans. Americans once knew better.

This Hiroshima anniversary, veterans who are critical of the atomic bomb should come forward so that we Americans will come to understand that members of the "Greatest Generation" do not march in lockstep on this issue.[1]

The reason Mr. Truman did not heed advice to explode the bombs over purely military targets, or in the absence of such targets, to explode the bombs close enough to Tokyo that all could see but not immediately be destroyed by the explosions, is something I've already addressed, at least in part, in a previous chapter. By the time the atomic bombs were dropped on Hiroshima and Nagasaki, the United States had, with few reservations, accepted and carried out a concept of Total War—a policy which said civilians, if not quite "legitimate targets," are sometimes "necessary targets."

But in spite of the fact that Sherman's "War is Hell" concept of war-fighting had already been accepted by American leaders as a military option that was sometimes expedient, there was still, at the beginning of the war, what seemed to have been a genuine reluctance to resort to the indiscriminate bombing of German cities. Consequently, both Churchill and Roosevelt had denounced the Nazi bombings of cities as odious and shocking. The British government had even gone so far as to announce that bombing nonmilitary targets was not part of its policy, no matter what the Nazi's might do. But we all know the "rest of the story." The Allies reneged, claiming they had a right to do so because Germany did not observe the same restrictions. So, after Germany's raid on Coventry, England in November 1940, the British Bomber Command was instructed to simply aim "at the center of a city." In other words, because the Third Reich, which was clearly an evil empire, didn't respect the principle of noncombatant immunity, the Allies adopted the evil empire's methods by breaking the same

---

[1] By permission of Uday Mohan and Leo Maley III, "Military: Hiroshima ... The Anniversary We Misremember," writing for History News Network, http://hnn.us/articles/167.html, July 30, 2001. History News Network is a web site of History News Service, http://www.h-net.org/~hns/.

rules, like their "he did it first" argument could somehow hold water.

In turn, the Allies' indiscriminate use of their own weapons bore much evil fruit in the "obliteration" or "saturation" bombings of Hamburg, Cologne and Berlin in 1942 and 1943, and Dresden in 1945. The bombings of Hamburg and Dresden created firestorms of unimaginable horror. As many as 135,000 people are believed to have been killed in the two days of raids on Dresden, which were considerably more than the deaths that would later be caused by the two atomic bombs themselves. Especially disturbing is the fact that thousands of those killed in Dresden were civilian refugees who were fleeing as a result of the Russian advance. This list would not be complete without mention of the estimated 100,000 people who died in the March 1945 incendiary raid on Tokyo. So it is clear that even before the rise of the Atomic Age, the United States' indiscriminate use of "conventional" weapons had already violated the principle of noncombatant immunity. Therefore, when Mr. Truman made his fateful decision to drop atom bombs on Hiroshima and Nagasaki, he was simply following the precedent set by the "War is Hell" policy that was, by then, already in place—a policy that had caused the deaths of thousands upon thousands of noncombatants.

This, then, is the backdrop against which Mr. Truman's decision to use nuclear weapons was made. So with this picture in mind, I ask the question once again, "Was Mr. Truman's decision right?" And once again, I respond, "No, it wasn't"

Many disagree. They think Mr. Truman's decision was prudent—the "greater good," and all that. On the other hand, many who agree with me that the indiscriminate use of weapons of war against noncombatants is wrong, do so for reasons far different from the one I am here defending.

Pacifists, peaceniks and other anti-war groups do not commonly believe there is anything about war that can be classified as "just." I believe these folks are wrong. However, in my defense of the Just War doctrine, I will not rubber stamp a "This is right!" slogan on everything my country has done with reference to armed conflict. In fact, I have been disappointed that too much talk from the non-pacifist's side of the fence seems to fall into the

"My country, right or wrong!" category. I am sorry to say I have even heard Christians talking about—and this was before the present occupation—turning Baghdad into a parking lot by an explosion of a strategically placed thermonuclear weapon a couple of thousand feet over the Iraqi capitol. Unfortunately, even New Testament Christians have bought into the indiscriminate killing of noncombatant men, women and children. Such thinking was a mistake in August 1945, and it is a mistake today. If this is to be the face of twenty-first century warfare, then I fail to see how Christians could ever hope to have any part in it.

By default, the activist believes that fighting for his country can't ever be wrong, while the pacifist, by default, believes war can't ever be right. Consequently, it is only the selectivist who must struggle with the facts which will determine whether a given war is just or not. If all this is true, and I believe it is, then it helps to focus the spotlight on one of the most difficult problems faced by the selectivist as he tries to make his decision of whether or not he'll participate in a given war: *Who has the authority to decide which wars are just or unjust?*

Who Has The Authority To Decide?

The activists will no doubt argue that chaos would reign if every individual in a country could make up his own mind whether or not to obey a certain law. What would be the result, they will argue, if everyone could decide which civil or domestic laws they would obey? Would not the result be anarchy and pandemonium? Yes, it would, but in making such an argument, activists are "mixing apples with oranges," so to speak. The question of war (i.e., whether it is right or wrong) is not to be confused with the Christian's obligation to obey every lawful ordinance of the State. In fact, the Bible says the Christian is under obligation to do just that.[2] Instead, the question is about morality itself, namely: *Can war be moral?* If the answer to this question is yes, then the

---

[2] See Rom. 13:1-7; 1 Pet. 2:13-17.

next question must be: *Under what circumstances is war moral?* Besides all this, and as has been previously noted, civil rulers do not have the authority to command that which God prohibits or, in turn, to forbid what He requires. Therefore, if a war does not have a just cause, then a Christian is prohibited from participating in it. In addition, if a war is just, but the Christian is called upon to do something in that war that is unjust, then he must refuse such an order.

Even so, and this is extremely important, the Christian is not permitted to determine which wars are just or unjust on the basis of his own *subjective* feelings. Rather, he endeavors to discover which wars are just or unjust on the basis of *objective* moral principles—principles that are, in turn, derived from the Bible itself. Thankfully, God has revealed in His word, by precepts and principles, the kinds of wars that would be just or unjust. The principles of justice and righteousness that unfold in the Bible, from beginning to end, are what permits the selectivist to determine whether a war in which his government has asked him to participate in is just or not. So, although it is true that the selectivist must discover the facts for himself, and this admittedly is not always easy (as we'll discuss in a moment), he is not without Biblical guidelines in assessing these facts once they are accumulated. Consequently, the selectivist is not an anarchist operating totally on his own. Instead, he makes his decision, if he's properly interpreted the Scriptures, with God's guidance.

I have argued thus far, and I think rightly so, that the pacifist and activist are wrong because they have incorrectly interpreted Scripture. But in doing so, I wish to make clear this caveat: *Even though he's come to the right conclusion concerning a Christian's right to participate in a just war, the selectivist can still, if he's not careful, involve himself in sin by participating in a war he has determined to be just, but isn't, or by doing something in an otherwise just war that is not, itself, just.* The remedy against such mistakes is a prayerful, diligent study of God's word coupled with a keen interest in national and international events.

But how, it is asked, can the Christian know *for sure* he isn't being lied to by his government or the media? That is, how does he know he's not simply being manipulated by his government or the media? Well, he'll never know "for sure," for nothing this side of heaven is for sure. Governments lie, and so do the media. So, living a righteous life in the real world is made even harder by the fact that lies are all too frequently told to advance the "good" or "righteousness" of some cause, even though the cause may actually be neither righteous nor good.

Therefore, when all is said and done, it all comes down to faith—that is, *what* do we believe in and *why* do we believe it? If there is convincing evidence that our government cannot be trusted to tell us the truth about the need to go to war, then how could an honest man conscientiously fight for a country in which he can place no trust, or for a cause he cannot trust is just?

Consequently, if the government to which one belongs has not made a habit of telling the truth about things like the need to go to war, then the Christian, in the absence of corroborating evidence, would be operating on blind faith, and blind faith isn't really faith at all. Real faith does not just believe something, it believes *in* something—that is, it trusts in what it believes.[3] Therefore, a government that repeatedly lies about such things to its citizens cannot be trusted, and a government that cannot be trusted is a government not worth fighting for.

Faced with such complexities, many opt for either pacifism or activism. However, a view isn't wrong just because it's difficult. After all, being a balanced Christian is the most difficult thing one can do in this sin-sick world. Balanced Christianity is salty, according to Matthew 5:13. As such, the only option open to the salty Christian is that of being a "selective conscientious objector"—a position that says the Christian must refrain from participating in any action or war that he deems, based upon his understanding of God's word, to be unjust. There is nothing easy about such a position. It will cause the selectivist to be at odds with both pacifists and activists, and sometimes the government itself. For if the government to which one belongs does not recognize the selectivist's conscience, then one can be shamed, imprisoned, or even worse.

---

[3] See Heb. 11:6.

Again, this between-a-rock-and-a-hard-place religion to which Christians ascribe is not easy, but it is the only way we can glorify God, His Son, and the Holy Spirit.

"Beware The Leaven Of The Pharisees"

Admittedly, Just War theory, although it derives ultimately from Scripture, is a tradition that has been developed by men. Therefore, just like the oral traditions of the Talmud, Just War doctrine, if we're not careful, can contradict and even displace what God has actually said in His word. Consequently, Just War doctrine, whatever it is perceived to be at any given moment in time, is but a tool (a grid, if you will) that aids its user in the discernment of correct and permissible actions involving the vagaries of life in a world marred by sin. In other words, first and foremost, Just War theory is a "systematic theology" of war that serves not only the individual, but the State as well. In fact, it is in the realm of statecraft[4] that its value can be especially appreciated, particularly in a time, like now, when war and the dark clouds of future wars lie menacingly on the horizon.

Contrary to what most people think, the Just War theory is not owned by a certain religious group or band of public intellectuals. Its teachings are not Catholic, Protestant, or whatever, and it is clericalism of the worst sort to suggest that religious leaders and public intellectuals "own" the Just War tradition in any singular way.[5] In fact, it is in its value to, and use by, government—whose primary function is to do justice—that the Just War theory has demonstrated itself to be of much help, even assisting, over the years of its existence, in the development of the moral consensus *for* or *against* war that is being reflected today in international discourse and law.

---

[4] By the use of the term "statecraft," I simply mean those things associated with the administration of government, namely, "politics," as this word is understood in its most classical meaning.

[5] For more on this, see George Weigel, "Moral Clarity in a Time of War" in *First Things*, December 2002.

Special Service Infers Special Obligations

So, if I am right about my understanding of Romans 13:1-7, and its implications for both citizen and government, then it is safe to say there is a realm of political discernment necessary to those whose vocation is public service that is not required of regular citizens. Similar to those who serve New Testament churches as pastors (viz., elders and bishops), watching out for the souls of those in their charge and who will one day give an accounting of their rule to God,[6] political leaders, who are obligated by God to uphold righteousness by doing acts of justice, will give an account to God for their actions. Consequently, the citizen is dependent upon his political leaders for moral clarity in a time of war, as well as all other times, for it is clear that the onus of responsibility falls squarely on the shoulders of the leaders.

This means, and just bear with me a moment here, that when a salty Christian sits on a jury, he will do everything within his power to arrive at a just verdict. If witnesses, under penalty of law, give perjured testimony, and such testimony becomes critical in determining either the guilt or innocence of the defendant, the blame for any unjust verdict does not pass to the jurors who, in all prudence, operated in good faith, nor to the court system that attempted, to the best of its ability, to operate justly. Likewise, a policeman, operating in good faith and exercising due diligence, does not commit a crime when he arrests an alleged lawbreaker for a crime he did not commit. Hopefully, such would be rectified in a court of law, but even then a policeman would not be held liable for the false arrest if, in the judgment of the court, he acted prudently. Furthermore, even if the courts did not correct the injustice of one falsely arrested for a crime, but instead found the falsely accused person guilty, guilt would not automatically pass to the court system as long as it exercised due process of law consistent with Biblical principles. However, anyone who gave false testimony, or who

---

[6] See Heb. 13:17.

manufactured, or in any way criminally tampered with evidence, would bear the guilt for any such travesty of justice.

By the same rule, no guilt would pass to a soldier who fights in what he, acting prudently, believes to be a just war, even when it is later discovered that the true reason for the war was clouded by lies. The issue, then, is this: *What would a reasonable and prudent man do?* This is all God has ever required, and this is true whether it has to do with faith in Him, or whether it has to do with the circumstances of life. Therefore, those who require absolute knowledge before they can act in a world tainted with sin must become ascetics, withdrawing from the very thing to which they are commanded to be both salt and light.[7] Such cannot be right, or so it seems to me.

Since the Christian must always sit in judgment upon the activities of his government, fully supporting it when it is right, but refusing to do so when it is wrong, the onus, as has already been said, is on public officials to be serious and truthful about what they say at all times, but especially at those times when they are asking citizens to consider war.

President Bush had some very tough decisions to make after 9/11. His political rivals in Congress who are "playing politics,"[8] are doing a disservice to those they have sworn to serve and protect. Without diminishing the death and destruction of those 9/11 attacks, they would simply pale in comparison with the explosion of a suitcase-size nuclear device in just one of our major cities. This, the Bush administration has told us, is "a real and present danger." Intelligence sources indicate suitcase-size nuclear weapons, which were developed by the former USSR, are presently being bought and sold on the Weapons-of-Mass-Destruction black market, which we are being led to believe can supply not just atomic weapons, but a deadly array of biological and chemical weapons as well. Consequently, when one or more of our major cities is disintegrated, gassed, or infected by one or more of these

---

[7] See Matt. 5:13-16.
[8] I use the word "politics" here in its degraded sense.

weapons (and don't forget that simultaneous attacks in "pairs" are the signature of al-Qaeda operations), it will then be too late to do anything about it.

In the meantime, American politicians not only continue to pooh-pooh the President's "Axis of evil" statement, but they are recklessly playing politics at the expense of America's security. Yes, the security of America is admittedly problematic; but this is due, in large part, to the unprecedented freedoms its citizens enjoy—freedoms ironically that many of the "nay-sayers" feel obligated to extend to those captured enemy combatants whose sworn purpose is to destroy them and these rights. But while claiming that the President has done nothing to protect us since 9/11, these hypocritical leaders, some of whom campaigned for the presidency themselves, have the unmitigated gall to turn around and criticize the President for practically everything he's done. Moral clarity in a time of war demands seriousness from public officials, and it's time for our public leaders, be they Republicans, Democrats, or Independents, to be deadly serious in what they are doing and saying, as the future peace and order of the United States depend on it. May God bless our leaders, particularly President Bush, with sobriety and wisdom in the days ahead, is my prayer. Further, I pray that the man or woman who follows him in office is not just some political hack simply featherbedding in office, but is serious about the president's solemn oath to protect America from its ememies.

I've taken the time to say all this because (1) the Christian's mind does not operate in a vacuum and (2) no matter how much we hold to the truth that God has provided in His Son and the Scriptures a once-and-for-all guide for moral conduct, we still have to struggle with the harsh realities of life in a fallen world. Honest, cogent thinking about war, even when it takes place within the framework of Just War theory, is assaulted by its gruesomeness, and such is made even worse by the introduction of nuclear weapons into the scheme of things. Admittedly, it has been the questions having to do with obliteration bombing and the use of nuclear weapons that have given me the most problems over the years when trying to defend or justify my position on warfighting. In fact, there was a time during the development of my current position when I tried to justify both. As you now know, I can no longer conscientiously do so. However, in thinking about the question of nuclear weapons, it is helpful to understand the history of their development and use over the years.

The Rise Of America's Nuclear Arsenal

The nuclear scientists who worked on the Manhattan Project, which began in 1942, did so because it was feared the Nazis were about to create their own atomic bomb. It was rumored they were working on one as early as 1939. Many of the scientists were European refugees who realized what a Nazi victory would mean for their native countries and for the rest of the world. Therefore, they did not accept the assignment to make the atomic bomb reluctantly, as has been reported in some quarters. In fact, they sought it out, even taking the initiative by urging President Roosevelt on with the critical importance of America matching the efforts of the Nazis. But as scientists they had no political power or following, so when it was learned in November, 1944, that the Germans had made little progress in their efforts, they were powerless to end the project they had helped to start. With their work largely completed, the technicians were in charge, and the politicians in charge of them. In other words, it was "a done deal," if you will. Albert Einstein said, "If I had known that the Germans would not succeed in constructing the atom bomb, I would not have lifted a finger."[9]

In March 1945, Henry Stimson, Secretary of War, informed President Roosevelt that "the bomb" would be ready for testing in July. On April 12, at the death of Mr. Roosevelt, Harry S. Truman became President and the decision whether or not to use the atomic bomb fell on his shoulders. On May 8, the Germans surrendered. During June, preparations were underway for the invasion of Japan, which was scheduled for November 1. On July 16 at 5:29:45 A.M., the Atomic Age officially began with the detonating

---

[9] Robert C. Battledore, *The Irreversible Decision: 1939-1950*, p. 38.

of the world's first atomic "device" at "Trinity" in the Nevada desert. That which had been conceived and created primarily to stop the Nazi war machine from achieving world conquest was no longer needed. However, having arrived, it was not about to be "disinvented."

From July 17 to August 2, Winston Churchill, Harry Truman and Joseph Stalin met at Potsdam, Germany. On July 26, in what has come to be called the Potsdam Proclamation, an ultimatum calling for Japan's unconditional surrender was issued. On July 28, Mr. Suzuki, the Japanese Prime Minister, announced he would "ignore" the offer. Consulting with a wide range of advisors, Mr. Truman made his fateful decision, and on the morning of August 6, an atomic bomb, nicknamed "Little Boy," exploded 1800 feet over the city of Hiroshima, Japan. Three days later, a second bomb, called "Fat Man" was exploded over the Japanese city of Nagasaki. Almost immediately, the Japanese announced their surrender. The war was over, and clearly the continued threat of nuclear weapons had hastened it, but the terror caused by an explosion and mushroom cloud on an August morning in 1945 had only just begun. It would grow to be something much more terrifying than the terror of the 12.5 and 20 kiloton bombs that had been dropped on Hiroshima and Nagasaki.

The immediate post-WW II years revealed that a Communist spy-ring was operating within the Manhattan Project, which was evidenced by the Soviet's startling August 16, 1949 detonation of their own atomic bomb. After an extensive investigation into the matter, Julius and Ethel Rosenberg were arrested in the summer of 1950. At the conclusion of their controversial trial, they were sentenced to death. Judge Kaufman, in his sentencing address, said in part:

> I consider your crime worse than murder. Plain deliberate contemplated murder is dwarfed in magnitude by comparison with the crime you have committed. In committing the act of murder, the criminal kills only his victim. The immediate family is brought to grief and when justice is meted out the chapter is closed. But in your case, I believe your conduct in putting into the hands of the Russians the A-bomb years before our best scientists predicted Russia would

perfect the bomb has already caused, in my opinion, the Communist aggression in Korea, with the resultant casualties exceeding 50,000 and who knows but that millions more of innocent people may pay the price of your treason. Indeed, by your betrayal you undoubtedly have altered the course of history to the disadvantage of our country.

On the evening of June 19, 1953, Julius Rosenberg and his wife Ethel were executed at Sing-Sing Prison in New York. By that time, there was no doubt our former allies, the Russians, had become our mortal enemies. Intending to stay ahead of the Soviets, Mr. Truman insisted on the development of a "super" or hydrogen bomb, which in turn resulted in the Arms Race/Cold War that plagued the world until the fall of the Soviet empire in the early 1990s. During this time, the United States' nuclear strategy changed several times. In the Dulles era of the fifties, the US and Allied policy was to threaten "massive retaliation." Echoing this, President Eisenhower, in his 1958 State of the Union address, spoke of "the prospect of virtual annihilation" which awaited the aggressor. The sixties brought nuclear stalemate and, in 1962, Robert McNamara, the Secretary of Defense, developed the "counter-force" concept, which said that retaliation would be limited to military targets. The key words under this plan became "flexible response" and "graduated response" which, it was argued, would help contain the use of nuclear weapons. However, many of the "experts" seemed to think containment was impossible, in that it was believed any use of nuclear weapons would inevitably escalate to a final conflagration. The seventies saw the heating up of the Cold War and a reverting to a Total War concept that culminated in the strategy of Mutually Assured Destruction (MAD) that dominated US nuclear policy for the next twenty-plus years.

In the midst of such thinking, President Reagan announced his Strategic Defense Initiative (SDI), a network of weapons designed to intercept and destroy ICBMs, rendering them "impotent and obsolete." This was an attempt to turn thinking toward the idea of effective defense rather than a MAD retaliation. Unfortunately, Mr. Reagan's initiative was met with all sorts of opposition (both

Left and Right), from scientists who questioned its feasibility, to those who objected to the "militarization of space," and those who expressed concern over eliminating the equilibrium that then existed between the two great superpowers. In response, Reagan argued that SDI was, indeed, feasible, and that the US would be willing to work jointly with the USSR to develop the system, going so far as to assure the Soviets we would even help them pay for its implementation.

A Historical Change In Thinking

Mr. Reagan's initiative was bold, to say the least, and it seems to have changed the course of nuclear history, moving it farther away from the morally indefensible policy of Mutually Assured Destruction that threatened nuclear holocaust. Although there must be no doubt that our world still lives under the shadow of those two mushroom clouds that rose so menacingly over the cities of Hiroshima and Nagasaki in those early days of August, 1945, the United States is now in the process of testing Reagan's vision of intercept weapons designed to "kill" intercontinental (ICBMs) and submarine launched (SLBMs) ballistic missiles. The program underwent change during the Bush 41 and Clinton presidencies, but it was Reagan's embrace of the idea that government, in order to meet its God-given responsibility, must at least try to develop a means of protecting its citizens from missile attacks that was now in play. And there can be no doubt that it was actually Reagan's vision that continued to spur the research and development of such defensive weapons. From the standpoint of Just War theory, Mr. Reagan's idea was a giant step in the right direction.

With the surprising dissolution of the old Soviet Union in 1991, many conservative pundits (viz., George Will, Irvin Kristol *et al.*) claimed that Reagan's SDI program, his buildup of the military, and his ideological crusade against Communism had delivered the knockout punch to a deteriorating Soviet system that had actually been on the ropes since the early 1980s. But it was SDI, they went on to say, that was "the key" to Reagan's winning strategy, as the Soviets had to realize there was no way their ailing system was going to be able to keep up with, in what promised to be the next arms race, the US's decisive techological advantange. From my own conservative standpoint, I believe this assessment is correct. Others, of course, wanted to give most of the credit to Mikhial Sergeyevich Gorbachev. Clearly, Mr. Gorbachev was an important player in these events—the right man at the right time, and all that. But anyone who thinks that one man inside the Soviet Union could have brought about the collapse of that evil empire is either a bit too naive about things in general, or too ignorant of the Soviet system in particular. No, it was strong pressure from the outside, weakness from within, and the failure of Communism itself that ushered in the fall of the Union of the Soviet Socialist Republic.

Today, those who continue to resist a defense-based initiative in the development of weapon systems do so for several clearly discernible reasons. First, there are those who believe war is immoral, period (viz., pacifists and other anti-war activists). To these people, war is simply not an option, even in self-defense. Second, there are those who believe the United States of America to be the locus of evil in the world today and, as such, a determined enemy of "peace" (viz., anti-American activists). These come with many different labels—Communists, Socialists, Islamists, *et cetera*. However, the "peace" these people are talking about is one in which their particular way of thinking is inflicted upon everyone else, which sounds to me a lot like totalitarianism. Third, there are those individuals who believe the nuclear stalemate between the two superpowers was a good thing, as it kept everyone in check. These folks long for the "good ol' days" of *détente*. Finally, there are those who honestly believe an effective defense against ICBMs and SLBMs is not possible. Put all these together and you continue to have a very effective vocal consensus in this country and around the world against what has been called "Star Wars" weaponry.

I believe it was most unfortunate that strategies for the use of nuclear weapons were spawned from the "War is Hell" philosophy that was used to justify the intentional targeting of civilians through the obliteration bombings of cities during World War II—a philosophy I've already identified as being immoral. Then, in the "tit for tat" arms race of the post-WW II years, massive thermonuclear weapons (viz., hydrogen bombs) were first tested and then implemented by both the US and the USSR. During those years, America even toyed with the idea of a vital first blow with nuclear weapons. Although such a plan appeared to be strategically sound, it was eventually rejected as immoral, or so it seemed. Since then, the United States has repeatedly said it would never start a nuclear war, which was interpreted by many to mean that the US would never employ a "first strike" use of nuclear weapons. However, this interpretation isn't correct, for the US has never rejected a first-use policy. In fact, the US has made it clear that if its conventional forces were ever being overrun by superior forces, it would consider using "theater size" nukes to even the odds. This policy was made clear to the Soviets who, at the height of the Cold War, had marshalled, along with the Warsaw Pact, overwhelming conventional military forces on the borders of Western Europe.

Additionally, the US has repeatedly denied that its no-first-strike policy would prevent it from employing a "preemptive strike," if and when necessary. A preemptive strike, of course, is nothing but a "first strike" launched against an enemy who is poised to strike, and which is done for the express purpose of keeping him from doing so. For example, if the US had known in 1941 that the attack on Pearl Harbor was imminent, they would have surely launched a preemptive strike on Yamamoto's carriers before they had the chance to launch their infamous attack. Such would have been viewed as both prudent and moral. Of course, the problem with a preemptive strike is that it clouds the point of who really started the war. This is why a preemptive strike, although it may be both prudent and moral, is seldom resorted to. When such is employed, it is usually frowned upon by bystanders and others not directly involved in the conflict.

More attractive, morally speaking, was a strategy of retaliatory strikes. This move, from first strike to retaliation, would give the US a capacity for deterrence, but not the ability to win a military victory. With such thinking came the idea that *any use* of nuclear weapons would be so terrible that every effort needed to be put forth to make sure these weapons of mass destruction were never used. During this time, there was the reintroduction and further development of the MAD strategy which said if you ever attack us with nuclear weapons, we will unleash on you a nuclear holocaust. Due to such thinking, the concept of civil defense, which prepared citizens to survive nuclear war during the 1950s and early 1960s, was eventually abandoned as useless, as nuclear war was thought to be so terrible that "surviving" no longer seemed like a "good thing." With this kind of thinking, nuclear weapons became useful for deterring others from attacking us, but not for actual use. Therefore, if the US was ever forced to use its nuclear weapons, those weapons would have failed in their purpose. Therefore, "the basic axioms of the nuclear age," according to Lawrence Freedman, were: "the impossibility of defense, the hopeless vulnerability of the world's major cities; the attraction of sudden attacks; and the necessity for retaliation."[10]

Today, with the old Soviet Union dissolved, many seem to think the threat of a nuclear holocaust no longer looms on the horizon. This is foolishness gone to seed. Yes, tensions seem to be reduced between East and West, but the United States is not the only superpower left in the world, as is foolishly being bantered about today. As General Colin Powell said when he was Chairman of the Joint Chiefs of Staff:

> No matter what happens in the Soviet Union, no matter how many walls fall down, no matter how many elections are held, or who the President may be, the Soviet Union will remain a military superpower—a nuclear military superpower with the ability, if not the intention, to destroy our way of life in 30 minutes.[11]

Even though the SALT I, SALT II and START treaties, along with other efforts, have reduced nuclear stockpiles by 75%, the Russians still have over 20,000 nuclear weapons in their arsenal, while the US has just over 10,000.

---

[10] *The Evolution of Nuclear Strategy*, 2nd edition, p. 44.
[11] Richard MacKenzie, "A Soldier Still on Guard," *InSight—On the News*, October 8, 1990, p. 17.

To give you a feel for what this looks like, you need to think of the 18 Ohio class nuclear-powered submarines that carry 50% of the United States' strategic nuclear weapons. Just one of these "Boomers," as they are called, has 24 silos loaded with a multiple warhead nuclear missile (viz., the Trident II D-5). The US, in compliance with the START treaty, has declared each of these missiles to contain 8 multiple independently targeted reentry vehicles (MIRVs), with each of these carrying a 300 to 475 kiloton warhead. This means that just one of the 192 MIRVs on a single Boomer (using an average kiloton figure) is more than 30 times more powerful than the 12.5 kiloton bomb dropped on Hiroshima. It seems clear that only a few of these would be required to "get the job done." Therefore, it is important to realize that the threat of nuclear holocaust is still a very real possibility in this troubled world in which we live.

My Conclusions Concerning Nuclear Warfare

As I've already said, nuclear weapons are not going to be disinvented. They are, and will continue to be, a very important part of the arsenals of both East and West. However, as we've described them here, such weapons are "unusable," in that if they ever are used they could very well start a conflagration that would cause the deaths of hundreds of millions of people. Consequently, and applying the Just War template, MAD strategy—although it worked insofar as the US and USSR never engaged in nuclear war (although we certainly got close during the Cuban missile crisis of 1962, as but only one example)—is immoral, in that it purposely targets the enemy's cities and the civilians who live in them. A deterrence is one thing, but a deterrence that can't be morally used is quite another. Therefore, the US has made it clear that, although it intends to keep its options open, it would, in fact, retaliate in force under certain circumstances. However, US nuclear strategy cannot be moral until and unless it concentrates its nuclear weapons on the enemy's military capabilities, rather than his cities. Executing such a strategy would not mean that civilians would not die, for they most certainly would die collaterally. But as long as the civilians were not being specifically targeted, guilt would not incur.

I am pleased the United States has renounced intentions of a war-winning nuclear strategy, making it clear it would never attack first with a supposed "knockout" nuclear strike. However, our government's talk of reserving the right to resort to preemptive strikes has led many to believe, and I think with good reason, that the US would strike first under certain circumstances. As misunderstood and threatening as preemptive strikes are, particularly in the case of nuclear weapons, I do not see how our government, or any government, for that matter, can morally give up this prerogative. In other words, to permit a nuclear attack on its citizens that could be prevented or at least diminished by a first strike would be a failure of the very thing governments are ordained by God to do. Further, it appears that the preemptive threat forced both superpowers to be careful of any movements that would alarm the other. After the Cuban missile crisis, where the US military, for the first and only time, went to Defcon-2, which is but one step away from actual war, both sides were even more careful not to do things that would unduly threaten the other side. It can be argued then that the ever present threat of a preemptive strike caused both sides to act more circumspectly. Therefore, I think my Just War cohorts who believe the US government must *unequivocally* renounce *all* "first strike" intentions err on this point.[12]

I am further pleased the United States has stopped development of bigger and more indiscriminate nuclear weapons, as such promised nothing but a further journey into the abyss of immorality and mutual destruction. During the fifties and sixties there had been talk of bombs so destructive that, once exploded, they might set off a chain reaction that would destroy the world. During those times, the US is known to have tested a 15-megaton hydrogen bomb, which is more than a thousand times more powerful than the bomb dropped on Hiroshima. The Soviets, on the other

---

[12] See Darrell Cole, *When God Says War Is Right*, 2002, pp. 130-133.

hand, announced they were developing a 100-megaton weapon. Much of this seems to have been madness, pure and simple, and I'm glad both sides finally came to their senses. But fairness demands it be pointed out that some of these weapons were experimented with due to the need to destroy deeply embedded weapons, not cities. Missiles back then were not as accurate as they are today, therefore it was necessary to have bigger weapons to get the job done.

Today, missile systems that are "smart" and extremely accurate are able to take out deeply embedded targets with much smaller warheads. This is why the MIRV warheads on those Trident II D-5s mentioned earlier are only in the 300-475 kiloton range. Clearly, we no longer need the big mega-tonnage once thought necessary. Therefore, the United States now has the ability in place to fully develop and implement a nuclear deterrent that is not inherently immoral, as was the MAD strategy. Instead of an immoral response to an enemy's immoral attack, which is all MAD promised, and which in turn is inherently unjust, we can accurately aim any response on our part only and directly at our enemy's military forces, which would effectively prohibit any victory on his part. Although enemy noncombatants would die in such a response, they would not be deliberately targeted, as they are under MAD strategy. Consequently, guilt for collateral deaths would not incur. This way, civilian deaths, even though they ultimately could be in the millions, play no part in our intended response. The good we would hope to accomplish by such a response would be to save our civilization. Millions of innocent civilians might be killed by our response, but we might save just as many, if not more, of our own innocent civilians. To me, this is a response that meets the requirements of Just War theory and is consistent with the principles of justice and righteousness taught in the Bible.

The Future

The US military has presently drifted away from simply planning a nuclear holocaust towards the possibility of nuclear warfighting. This, as I see it, is a good trend, for it should be apparent that unusable weapons, whether they be nuclear or conventional, are immoral, and are so precisely because they are, in fact, unusuable. In other words, if we are going to spend bundles of money to make and maintain nuclear weapons, there ought to be a moral scenario where they may be righteously used. As the U.S. continues to develop technologically, it may eventually be possible for the military to develop a shield that protects us from ICBMs fired at us by other nations, rogue states, and terrorist organizations. Such technology, although controversial, is something I believe ought to be pursued. Unfortunately, up to this point, there have been no clear-cut rules, no guiding moral principles, behind the aforementioned trend. So far, all that has happened has arisen from either accidents or technology (viz., more accurate guidance systems meant we could use smaller warheads against hardened sites) or the inarticulated, but nonetheless, real horror of actually doing what our nuclear weapons are capable of doing, which is creating a thermonuclear holocaust of gargantuan proportions. Estimates during the Cold War said that a Soviet attack against America would kill sixty-five percent of our people. Consequently, I agree with Joseph P. Martino's conclusion on page 282 of his excellent and thought-provoking book, *A Fighting Chance: The Moral Use of Nuclear Weapons*:

> We have a lot of lost time to make up. We can only pray that we will be granted the additional time necessary. We must begin by rejecting both defeatism ("It can't be done!") and moral obtuseness ("It shouldn't be done!"). Then we must undertake the hard task we have neglected all the years since Hiroshima, those of learning how to use nuclear weapons morally, and of building weapons we can use in good conscience should the need arise.

Clearly, the moral use of nuclear and thermonuclear weapons remains a problem for those who hold to any form of Just War theory. Strategies for using such weapons that derive from the "War is Hell" World War II doctrine of obliteration bombing, where the goal was to attack large areas of cities, or even whole cities, will always be unacceptable to those who believe all aspects of war-fighting, in order to be morally acceptable, must be consistent with the principles of Justice and Righteousness expounded in the Bible.

We are, I believe, at a critical juncture. The moment requires critical thinking about, and assessment of, the way we, as a people, have come to think of the issues associated with war-fighting. If we do not rise to the occasion and totally abandon the concept of purposely targeting civilians, then I fear that we, as a nation, will be relegated to the dustbin of history. Remember, as Proverbs 14:34 says, "Righteousness exalts a nation, but sin is a reproach to any people."

Chapter 9

What About The United Nations?

In the aftermath of Hiroshima and Nagasaki, a new type of pacifism has arisen which asks the question of how an all-out nuclear war could ever be considered morally acceptable, since it would obviously inflict more injury on the world than it could possibly correct. Although this new pacifism has been identified by several names (viz., "relative pacifism" and "neopacifism"), it has come to be called "nuclear pacifism." The moral principle invoked by nuclear pacifists is the one that says it is never right to cause more injury than one seeks to mend, regardless of the provocation. Convinced that all-out nuclear war cannot serve a rational or moral end, they argue that not only would such a war be immoral, but that even a defense based upon waging such a war is immoral, and further that the continued development of such weapons of mass destruction is also immoral.

But if the truth be told, many nuclear pacifists aren't "pacifists" at all, at least in the true sense of the word. Their concern fixates on the "terror" of nuclear weapons, and all this quite apart from any convictions about armies, navies, and the role of government. In fact, they still want policemen to protect them and their loved ones, and they still want their rulers to stand up to enemy states. All they are advocating is a new and special limit on the fighting of wars. Therefore, they are really supporters of the Just War doctrine. In contrast to this, historical pacifism views war as not only a social evil, but a sin. Therefore, consistent, honest pacifists wouldn't be caught dead arguing against nuclear weapons on practical grounds like their destructiveness, expense, et cetera, which are in turn things nuclear pacifists argue all the time.

Be that as it may, religious/philosophical pacifists have largely co-opted the nuclear pacifist movement, seeing it as a more viable way to advance their agenda, which, in the end, is to outlaw war altogether. In truth, historical pacifists have no more business in the nuclear arms argument than a Protestant minister does at a Roman Catholic retreat for clergy or a Democrat does at a Republican caucus. Even so, pacifists over the years have furiously entered into the campaign to bring about, to one degree or another, the total elimination of nuclear arms from the arsenal of the United States and other NATO countries. During the Cold War, nuclear disarmament, as advanced by the "peaceniks" and other anti-war advocates, was the ever-present, ongoing argument that said it was, in fact, "Better to be Red than dead!" Today, more than half a century after the start of the Cold War, this argument is still with us in the fairly common held idea that modern warfare is so terrible that it must be avoided at all cost, even when one of these costs is justice itself.

Enter just here the United Nations, which by charter is committed to the peaceful resolution of all disputes and conflicts between states and peoples. Under such a mandate, justice is sacrificed on the altar of "Peace at any price." However, God's word makes it clear that peace is an enterprise of justice.[1] The United Nations, although touted by its adherents as "our last, best hope for peace," has never brought about peace, and it never will. Those who use such slogans are like chickens with their heads cut off (all reflex and no reason), who fail to realize that the United Nations, by virtue of its own charter, will always be forced to genuflect to raw power, rather than effect true justice. Who today, but headless chickens, could argue that the existence of the United Nations has even begun to eliminate the need of warfare as a means of defending oneself from aggression? The world, due to its fallenness, is a very dangerous place, and even more so today than when the United Nations came into existence on October 24,

---

[1] See Isa. 32: 17 and note that the Hebrew word translated "righteousness" can also be translated as "justice."

1945. As we think about the subject at hand, I believe it is beneficial to understand just how dangerous the world's present trust in the United Nations really is.

The New Babel

In Genesis 11:1-9, we learn of a human race, united in both language and purpose, that had determined to build a tower in the Plain of Shinar. The construction of this tower was to serve as a monument to human achievement. The attitude of its builders was indicative of those who had rejected God as their Creator. Dr. Merrill F. Unger, in his well-known dictionary of the Bible, identifies the basic motivation underlying the entire project as "God-defying disobedience and pride" (Unger's Bible Dictionary, p. 114). Addressing this on page 6 of his book, *New Age Globalism*, H. Edward Rowe wrote:

> We must not miss the central warning that resounds through the corridors of the long centuries to our time. The tower builders structured a mighty global organization, independent of God. They dedicated it to the establishment of a human unity which would secure them against the prospect of being scattered apart throughout the world.

The Bible, of course, teaches us that God was very much displeased with their effort and, as a result, He "confounded their language" and "scattered them abroad," which was the very thing they were trying to prevent!

Unfortunately, the descendants of the Babel builders are still with us today. Their plan for creating a "global society" is evident in their various writings. In *Humanist Manifesto II*, under the heading, "World Community," we read:

> We deplore the division of humankind on nationalistic grounds. We have reached a turning point in human history where the best option is to transcend the limits of national sovereignty as to move toward the building of a world community... We look to the

development of a system of world law and a world order based upon transnational federal government.

Elsewhere in the same document, we read, "What more daring a goal for humankind than for each person to become, in ideal as well as practice, a citizen of a world community." According to this manifesto, "No deity will save us: we must save ourselves."

As a result of the 1944 Dumbarton Oaks Proposal, as well as the 1945 Yalta and San Francisco Conferences, the United Nations Charter came into force on October 24, 1945. On December 14,1946, the U.N. accepted a gift of $8.6 million from John D. Rockefeller, Jr. to buy the eighteen acres of land on New York's East River upon which the current U.N. building sits. The next year, the U.S. Congress approved a $65 million interest-free loan to finance the construction of the glass, stone, and steel tower dedicated to the enshrinement of "collective security." Between 1945 and 1987 alone, the United States contributed $17 billion of the estimated $87 billion spent by this organization. During that time the so-called "nonaligned nations," which make up the majority of the United Nations delegations, voted the communist line fully 85 percent of the time in the General Assembly. So, like the Tower of Babel before it, the United Nations, worshipping the false gods of man, all in the name of unity and security, represents a denial of the Lordship of Jesus Christ, the Creator, Sustainer, and Savior of the world. The builders of this modern-day Tower of Babel place man above God and their Almighty Super State above man.

"The initial optimism with which the world was aglow after World War II has long since faded before the gruesome reality of some three-hundred plus civil and regional wars that have raged since 1945, including Korea and Vietnam."[2] In addition, during these past fifty-seven years, there have been no shortages of bombings, assassinations, hijackings, terror attacks and other

---

[2] Fred Bruning, "The U.N. At Forty," *The Courier Journal*, September 22, 1985, p. D1.

such demonstrations of man's inhumanity to his fellowman. Although the recent "defeat" of communism and the "one-hundred hour" war to "liberate" Kuwait has bolstered the optimism of some, the 9/11 terror attacks on America grimly demonstrate that these were nothing to get excited about.

The Underpinnings Of Both Projects

Obviously, then, both projects—the tower on the Plain of Shinar and the one on New York's East River—convey significant information about the people they represent. Dr. Rowe, who I mentioned previously, in identifying these indicators as they relate to the Tower of Babel, wrote:

- *Philosophically*, it represents belief in the priority of the materialistic realm over the spiritual.

- *Theologically*, it involves a substitution of a false god for the True and Living God.

- *Psychologically*, it implies confidence in the achievement of security by means of a global man-made unity.

- *Educationally*, it means problem solution based on adequacy of man rather than guidance of God.

- *Administratively*, it exhibits an unfounded assurance of the self-sufficiency of organized man without reliance on God.

- *Anthropologically*, it proclaims the glories of human pride and self-aggrandizement.

Of course, one has little difficulty applying these same indicators to the United Nations.

The builders of the Tower of Babel were determined to build a tower "whose top may reach unto heaven." It is interesting, then, that Alvin Toffler, on page 308 of his popular book, *The Third Wave*, wrote:

Globalism presents itself as more than an ideology serving the interests of a limited group: Precisely as nationalism claimed to speak for the whole nation, globalism claims to speak for the whole world. And its appearance is seen as an evolutionary necessity—a step closer to a "cosmic consciousness" that would embrace the heavens as well.

Quoted in an official brochure of the World Federalists Association, the late Bertrand Russell summed up the case for "One-World-ism" with these words: "Science has made unrestricted national sovereignty incompatible with human survival. The only possibilities are now world government or death."[3] Lord Beveridge of England put it this way: "World peace requires world order. World order requires world law. World law requires world government."[4] Way back in June, 1976, former presidents of the National Education Association (an organization that continues to be one of the UN's strongest supporters) had this to say about educators and their role in developing a new world order or "global community": "It is with...sobering awareness that we set about to change the course of American education for the twenty-first century by embracing the ideals of global community, the equality and interdependence of all peoples and nations, and education as a tool to bring about world peace."[5] The title of this document is even more interesting when one considers that on January 30, 1976, the World Affairs Council announced the *Declaration of Interdependence*, which was signed by 32 U.S. Senators and 92 U.S. Representatives in Washington, D.C., and read in part, "Two centuries ago our forefathers brought forth a new nation; now we must join with others to bring forth a new world order." This document further stated, "To establish a new world order...it

---

[3] *World Peace Through World Law With Justice...Developing New Avenues To World Order*, 1101 Arlington Blvd., Suite S-119, Arlington, Va. 22209.

[4] Phillip D. Butler, "Parliamentarians for World Order," in *The Canadian Intelligence Service*, Vol. 33, No.5, May 1983, p. 41.

[5] From the Forward to A Declaration of Interdependence: Education for a Global Community, a summary report of the NEA Bicentennial Program, an NEA publication dated June 26, 1976.

is essential that mankind free itself from the limitations on national prejudice..." And again: "We call upon all nations to strengthen the United Nations...and other institutions of world order..."[6]

So, we ought not to be surprised that former ambassador to the United Nations, and former president, George H. Bush, who was between 1977 and 1979 a director of the U.S. Council on Foreign Relations,[7] would fight the first Persian Gulf War under the aegis of a United Nations Security Council mandate. On January 29, 1991, during his now infamous State of the Union/New World Order address, Bush 41 made it clear that the fate of Kuwait was not the main issue:

What is at stake is more than one small country, it is a big idea—a new world order, where diverse nations are drawn together in common cause to achieve the universal aspirations of mankind: peace and security, freedom, and the rule of law. Such is a world worthy of our struggle, and worthy of our children's future.

Then, in his March 6, 1991 address to Congress commemorating the successful conclusion of the Persian Gulf War, Bush 41 said:

Until now, the world we've known has been a world divided—a world of barbed wire and concrete block, conflict and cold war. Now, we can see a new world coming into view. A world in which there is the very real prospect of a new world order. A world where the United Nations, freed from cold war stalemate, is poised to fulfill the historic vision of its founders.

Then, when the wounded-pride dictator of Iraq lashed out against his own citizens, we strictly refused to intervene. Why? We

---

[6] In A. Ralph Epperson, *The Unseen Hand*, p. 371.

[7] A body of so-called "wise men" who have dominated foreign policymaking by the United States government since before World War II, and who came up with the idea of the United Nations.

could not support the Kurds and Shias, we were told, because doing so was not part of the United Nations mandate. But now more than a decade later, and with the son of Bush 41 in the White House, we have been shown the gruesome pictures of Iraqi Kurds, defenseless men, women and children, who Saddam Hussein unmercifully gassed in northern Iraq—people we were told we could not defend because we didn't have a UN mandate.

I am not so naive as to think Bush 41 actually allowed himself and the United States of America to be used by the United Nations. In fact, it was most definitely the other way around. Bush 41 effectively manipulated the United Nations apparatus to do what he wanted it to do. The United States had, and still has, strategic interests in that very unstable part of the world, and Saddam Hussein, it was agreed on by all who took part in the first Persian Gulf War, needed to be taught that he could not exercise his military muscle without some serious consequences. But much to the chagrin of Bush 41, who Saddam Hussein outlasted in office by a decade, the diabolical dictator of Iraq was a much more determined, ruthless, and powerful tyrant than he thought.

Even so, there must be no mistake that the real military might that was exercised in the first Persian Gulf War belonged to America—not NATO, not Britain, and certainly not the United Nations. When it was all said and done, the United Nations did what Bush 41 wanted it to do. Many argued then, as some are arguing now in view of current events, that this was a good thing because our cause was just then and it's just now. Fine, some would say, because all's well that ends well. This may sound pretty good, but suppose for a moment that the action undertaken had not been just, and then you will begin to understand the point I am trying to make here: *The danger with one-world-government is that it can be, and more than likely will be, used by imperialists and tyrants to manipulate the greater masses for the so-called "greater good"—something that would not be good at all, but evil.* With this thought in mind, it is interesting to know that Isaiah Bowman, at a U.S. Council on Foreign Relations meeting in May, 1942, actually suggested a United Nations type organization as a way for the U.S. to exercise its strength to assure "security" in the world, and at the same time "avoid conventional forms of imperialism."[8]

When I originally wrote some of this material in January of 2003, I could not help seeing the irony of a united mankind, in the name of "collective security," and under the auspices of the United Nations, assembling itself, once again, in the very place where mankind, because of an ungodly and ill-conceived unity platform, was originally scattered by God. Unlike many pundits, I applauded George W's willingness to "go it alone." His "You're either with us or against us" remarks, although vilified by many as arrogance, actually reflected the words of Jesus, who said in Matthew 12:30, "He who is not with me is against me; and he who does not gather with Me scatters abroad." I know Jesus was God incarnate and therefore could have said this without the charge of arrogance being attached to it. But instead of seeing these words as representing arrogance, why can't we understand them for the common sense truth they represent? Those in the international community who harbor terrorists and give financial succor to them are against us, not for us. Those who become friends with our enemies quite logically become our enemies. Therefore, if the many nations of the world can't agree that terrorists and those who aid them need to be brought to the bar of justice, particularly when this necessarily involves war, then they too are enemies of the United States of America. Does this mean we declare war on all our enemies? Certainly not! But when our enemies direct their assaults against us, they can expect to be attacked in order that justice might be done. So to those who naively believe that war is never the answer, Biblical-based reason says, "Get real!"

There is, of course, only one way for the world to be united, and it has absolutely nothing to do with governments' exercise of the sword—whether this be in courts of law or on the battlefields of war. The great apostle Paul taught that this unity or "oneness"

---

[8] Memorandum T-A25, May 20, 1942, CFR, War-Peace Studies, Hoover Library on War, Revolution, and Peace, Stanford, CA.

can only be recognized by those who understand that Jehovah, their Creator, demands they kiss His Son in obedience.[9] Yes, nationalism is, according to Acts 17:26b, ordained by God, and with this ordination comes duties and responsibilities that cannot be abridged by man's devices without serious consequences. But ultimately, the solutions to mankind's problems are of Divine, not man-made and ill-conceived, origin. The sovereignty of every nation is to be respected as its people seek the Lord.[10] It is He, and He alone, who is the Savior of humankind. His earthly kingdom, the church of Christ, has already been established, and "all nations [must flow] unto it" to be saved.[11] It is in this everlasting spiritual kingdom, and not the United Nations, that men out of every nation on the face of the earth will "beat their swords into plowshares, and their spears into pruninghooks."[12] And it is only in this spiritual relationship, according to Micah 4:3, that "nation shall not lift up sword against nation, neither shall they learn war any more."

Obviously, then, the United Nations, a supra-national organization, is not, nor could it ever be under its current charter, a vehicle for true peace—that is to say, "peace with justice." It is, according to Romans 13:1-7, the duty of individual governments, not the United Nations, to serve and protect its citizens. Saying this does not mean I'm against alliances or coalitions, particularly when common interests so dictate. However, the direction in which the United Nations is headed is not a coalition or alliance of nations where each nation retains its own sovereignty, directing its own affairs and actions. Instead, in its present state, it is a man-made vehicle for world government that cannot, by its very nature, have the best interest of American citizens at heart. For this reason, I am against it. As a vehicle of debate and discussion, and for genuine consensus building, it has some value. But as a decision making body, and with the World Court under its auspices,

---

[9] See Acts 17:22-31; Psa. 2:12.
[10] See Acts 17:26-27.
[11] See Isa. 2:2-3.
[12] Isa. 2:4.

and with an army of so-called "peace-keepers" directly under its command, the sovereignty of all nations, including ours, will be sacrificed on the altar of "universal peace." Remember this: *a peace without Justice and Righteousness, even if it were universal in scope, would not be worth having.*

Chapter 10

Was The War In Iraq Just?

The war in Iraq needs to be viewed as a subset of the larger "War on Terror" that began in response to the September 11, 2001 sneak attacks that took the lives of thousands of Americans in New York City, Washington, D.C. and rural Pennsylvania. It is unfortunate that many do not see it this way. This chapter is designed to help these folks see the error of their way.

Although most who died on 9/11 were innocent civilians whose only crime was to get up and go to work that fateful morning, to their enemies they were "infidels" who deserved to die horrible and fiery deaths. Consequently, when both towers of the World Trade Center collapsed, Osama bin Laden gloated over the deaths of three thousand innocent people who had become the objects of his hatred of America. To bin Laden and a multitude of Muslims around the world who celebrated this so-called "glorious deed," these innocent civilians were not just murdered horribly, but they were effectively robbed of what they were on that frightful day: workers from more than eighty-six countries simply doing their jobs in the World Trade Center and the Pentagon *and* businesspeople, retirees, children, and grandparents traveling coast to coast on four airliners. Instead, they were simply "the enemy."[1] Consequently, they were stripped of their status as noncombatants—a status that would have provided them the protection against intentional targeting and assault provided by any reading

---

[1] Elisabeth Bumiller, "Bin Laden, on Tape, Boasts of Trade Center Attacks; U.S. Says It Proves His Guilt," *New York Times*, December 14, 2001, pp. 1, B4.

of just war theory, whether it be the reading advocated by Western culture or the Islamic world.

But before proceeding any further it needs to be pointed out that although there are similarities and overlaps in Western and Islamic just war theories, the assimilation is not as clear as some think. For example, Bassam Tibi, a Muslim and professor of international relations who has written on Islam, war, and modernity has said:

> [The] Western distinction between just and unjust wars linked to specific grounds for war is unknown in Islam. Any war against unbelievers, whatever its immediate ground, is morally justified. Only in this sense can one distinguish just and unjust wars in Islamic tradition. When Muslims wage war for the dissemination of Islam, it is a just war.... When non-Muslims attack Muslims, it is an unjust war. The usual Western interpretation of jihad as a "just war" in the Western sense is, therefore, a misreading of this Islamic concept.[2]

This is not to say that there are no moral restraints on the conduct of war within classic or traditional Islam. There are, but these restraints reflect more upon the appeal to a warrior's honor than to a soldier's sense of justice. This is a point that Michael Ignatieff makes in his book *The Warrior's Honor*.[3] He says that the intentional slaughter of civilians, according to the warrior's honor code, is a dishonorable thing. Nevertheless, he admits that this idea is a difficult one to impress upon those trained in the rhetoric of modern Islamic jihad.[4] Traditionally, the primary goal of the Islamic warrior when fighting against unbelievers was to force them to submit to Islam, not to destroy them. However, this goal has been lost in modern Islamist fundamentalism. Therefore, although it is fair to say that classical Islam placed certain moral

---

[2] "War and Peace in Islam," in Terry Nardin, ed., *The Ethics of War and Peace*, 1996, pp. 128-45, in Jean Bethke Elshtain, *Just War Against Terror: The Burden of American Power in a Violent World*, 2003, p. 131.

[3] 1997, p. 147.

[4] See Tibi's statement in Elshtain, *Just War Against Terror*, p. 133.

restraints on military conduct that were similar to our Western just war theory, even when these wars were fought against non-Muslims, when one turns to contemporary discussions of this issue among Muslims, "one is struck with the scarcity of *jus in bello* [i.e., just conduct in war] materials."[5]

Consequently, there is a crisis within Islam today that has been described as a battle between *Islam*, which reflects the classical view, and *Islamism*, which mirrors the radical fundamentalist world view we see being manifested today. Will the Islamic moderates, who do in fact have a rich tradition of tolerance and respect for human life, win the battle for their religion, or will the radical fundamentalists win the day? If the latter, then radical jihadists will continue to be hunted down and destroyed. In the process, many good, honest and peaceful Muslims will suffer in the War on Terror—a war that will eventually escalate into a battle of momentous import. In fact, and in anticipation of the radical fundamentalists' continued influence within Islam, some have already started calling the current War on Terror "World War IV."[6] Thus, the more virulent Islamism becomes, the more difficult life will be for both moderate Muslims and the rest of us so-called "infidels." Consequently, although moderate Muslims, who by every estimation remain the overwhelming majority within Islam today, feel threatened and intimidated by the jihadis (radical fundamentalists) in their midst, they must, for their own good, begin to speak out against and resist those who have hijacked their religion.

With this said, the stark contrast between "us" (viz., the West, including moderate Muslims) and "them" (viz., the militant jihadis) should now be quite clear: On one side we have the unequivocal, non-nuanced condemnation of an intentional attack using vehicles of peaceful travel (viz., commercial airlines) against buildings in which commerce was conducted and people worked to

---

[5] John Kelsay, *Islam and War: A Study in Comparative Ethics*, 1993, p. 45.

[6] See a statement made by ex-CIA director James Woolsey to a group of college students at the University of California at Los Angeles on April 2, 2003, identifying the cold war as World War III and the War on Terror as World War IV.

support their families. On the other side, we have the reveling in, and joyous celebration of, vicious, heartless attacks against innocent non-combatants. The difference is both fundamental and telling, and how we describe the 9/11 attacks determines how we speak of the attackers. In other words, were the 9/11 hijackers murderers, as we say, or martyrs, as they say?

To glorify as martyrs those whose primary purpose was, and is, to murder as many unarmed civilians as possible, is to foist upon the civilized world a morally distorted world view—a view that would provoke, if the West held to the same view, turning the cities and villages of the Muslim world into a lifeless mass of rubble ("pounding the rubble," as some say). The awesome, unmatched superiority of the West's military might is not questioned by anyone who is still in his right mind. Therefore, it is clear that the West, headed by the United States of America, has the capacity to turn the Muslim world into a "parking lot," if it so desired. Thankfully, and I'm sure much to the relief of millions upon millions of non-jihadi Muslims around the world, the West has no such desire, and this is the very difference a Biblical world view makes—a world view that entertains no thoughts of enslaving or eradicating the Muslim world. Thus, in his speech to the nation on September 20th, 2001, President Bush—although already being criticized in the Muslim world and the European media for a slip of the tongue in an impromptu press conference soon after the attacks, where he said, in part, "...this crusade, this war on terrorism, is going to take a while"—made it crystal clear that the War on Terror was not a total war, a holy war, or even an attack on Islam. To Muslims everywhere, he said officially and distinctively:

> We respect your faith. It's practiced freely by many millions of Americans, and by millions more in countries that America counts as friends. Its teachings are good and peaceful, and those who commit evil in the name of Allah blaspheme the name of Islam. The terrorists are traitors to their own faith, trying, in effect, to hijack Islam itself. The enemy of America is not our many Muslim friends; it is not our

many Arab friends. Our enemy is a radical network of terrorists, and every government that supports them.[7]

Having worked and lived in other places of the world, I want to say that I have Muslim acquaintances, some of whom I count as friends, who have on numerous occasions gone out of their way to demonstrate kindness and civility to me. In fact, some of the kindest deeds bestowed upon me and my wife have been performed by Muslims—deeds that ultimately aided me in preaching the gospel in difficult times and places. Furthermore, those Muslims who aren't my personal friends are, as the Bible so clearly teaches me, my neighbors.[8] Consequently, I am obligated to do unto my Muslim neighbors as I would have them do unto me.[9] So, when I hear Christians talking about the need to make Baghdad, Kabul, Teheran, or Damascus "a parking lot," it sorely vexes my spirit. This is no way for a Christian, whether he be a civilian or soldier, to be thinking or talking, and Christians who have crossed over to the dark side in my presence have been rebuked for such un-Christlike thinking.

These personal observations are not, as some might think, a digression from the subject before us. Instead, they are an appropriate contextualization of the subject, for in attempting to defend what I believe to have been a just war in Iraq, I cannot deny the truths taught in God's word. I cannot attempt a justification of the Iraq War by denying *who* and *what* I am: a Christian *first* and an American *second*. Consequently, any justification of the war with Iraq must be consistent with the New Testament's teaching on the Christian's duty to neighbor and government, along with the government's God-given obligations to do justice and uphold righteousness.

---

[7] "Address to a Joint Session of Congress, September 20, 2001," in *Our Mission and Our Moment: Speeches Since the Attacks of September 11*, 2002, pp. 9-15.

[8] See Lk. 10:25-37.

[9] See Matt. 7:12.

As the Bible says in Proverbs 14:34, "Righteousness exalts a nation; but sin is a reproach to any people." This means that the righteous acts of Christians are not only important to the personal salvation of Christians themselves, but to the preservation of our nation as well. What happens, then, when the salt loses its savor? Jesus clearly answered this question when He said, in Matthew 5:13, that it was good for nothing but to be cast out and trodden under the feet of men.

To permit a murder to occur when it could have been prevented is morally wrong. To allow a rape when one could have deterred it is an evil thing. To watch an act of cruel abuse of a child without stepping in to end it is morally inexcusable. God's word says, "Anyone, then, who knows the right thing to do and fails to do it, commits sin."[10] A man who will not protect his wife and children against a violent intruder, even when he believes the Bible prohibits him from doing so (as one who is a consistent, total pacifist would have to do), fails them miserably. And although it is true that a pacifist who rightly defended his wife and children would sin by doing so, in that he would be violating his own conscience,[11] he would, nevertheless, be sinning if he didn't. Therefore, the pacifist's "damned if you do; damned if you don't" dilemma should amply demonstrate the importance of getting this issue right. God's word, when properly interpreted, does not create such moral dilemmas.

Likewise, any government that has the means to defend its citizens against a foreign aggressor and fails to do so is morally delinquent. Even as justice demands a life for a life in capital crimes, the same logic can be extended to the unjust actions of nations, and this means that a government has a moral duty to take punitive actions against an aggressor nation, with Hitler being a notable case in point. It would have been morally wrong for the Allied Forces (in this case a group of aggrieved nations) not to have re-

---

[10] Jas. 4:17, NRSV.
[11] See Rom. 14:22-23.

sisted Nazi Germany. To ordain government, as God clearly did,[12] and then prohibit it from doing what it has been ordained to do, would deny the very right of the government to exist at all, which would, in turn, be a direct contradiction of what the Bible said about God-ordained government. Therefore, the pacifist position cannot be right!

Thus, instead of making the government's work harder by attempting to prohibit its God-given right to use deadly force, Christians should be willing to uphold the government's righteous hand as it does justice.[13] However, I do not believe one's citizenship should ever interfere with the Christian's duty to obey God rather than men.[14] Consequently, if the justification for the war with Iraq was invalid, then it would have to be condemned by every right thinking Christian. In other words, there are times when a Christian must refuse to serve his country, and that if he didn't do so, he would be involving himself in sin. If one's government embarks upon an unjust war, the Christian could not, without sin, actively participate in it. This, then, goes to the very heart of the question: *Was the Iraq War just, or not?*

Perhaps you haven't picked up on it yet, but I have been referring to the Iraq War in the past tense. For like President Bush, I believe the war with Iraq is over, and that we won. Therefore, and despite what the critics continue to say, the "Mission Accomplished" sign that stood behind President Bush aboard the *USS Abraham Lincoln* when he gave a speech on the flight deck to returning sailors, Marines and airmen on May 1, 2003, ought to have been understood in the context of the Iraq War which, with the fall of Baghdad and the dissipation of any organized resistance from Saddam's forces, was a clear victory for Coalition Forces. However, Bush said in that speech that "The Battle of Iraq is one victory in a war on terror that began on September 11th, 2001, and still goes on." He went on to say:

---

[12] See Rom. 13.
[13] See 1 Pet. 2:14; Tit. 3:1; Rom. 13:1-7.
[14] See Acts 5:29.

Any person involved in committing or planning terrorist attacks against the American people becomes an enemy of this country, and a target of American justice. Any person, organization, or government that supports, protects, or harbors terrorists is complicit in the murder of the innocent, and equally guilty of terrorist crimes.

Making it clear that the United States would not hesitate to use force against other terrorist threats, he said:

The use of force has been and remains our last resort. Yet all can know, friend and foe alike, that our nation has a mission. We will answer threats to our security and we will defend the peace.

He further said:

The advance of human freedom, the great achievement of our time and the great hope of every time, now depends on us. Our nation, this generation, will lift the dark threat of violence from our people and our future. We will rally the world to this cause by our efforts, by our courage. We will not tire, we will not falter, and we will not fail.

Finally, Mr. Bush shifted into the first person, and said:

I will not forget the wound to our country and those who inflicted it. I will not yield, I will not rest, I will not relent in waging this struggle for freedom and security for the American people. The course of this conflict is not known, yet its outcome is certain. Freedom and fear, justice and cruelty, have always been at war, and we know that God is not neutral between them.

With these words, the *Bush Doctrine* was clearly and succinctly articulated.

However, the purpose of this chapter is not to defend the War on Terror, *per se*, which I think most right-thinking people already believe to be a just war. The task, instead, is to show why the Iraq War was just. This, it seems, is the more difficult position to defend, even in the minds of many who acknowledge the legitimacy of the larger War on Terror. To these, the Iraq War is troubling primarily because they have not been able to see the linkage of Iraq to the events of 9/11.

I'll have more to say about this linkage in a moment, but before doing so, let me emphasize this point: The Iraq War is over. Saddam's military was soundly defeated and his government is no more. But although we clearly *won the war*, we have not yet *secured the peace*. The guerrilla war that is now underway in Iraq, a war that involves some leftovers from the Saddam regime (Baathists and the like), insurgents from outside Iraq, and hard-core terrorists (from Algeria, Tunisia, Egypt, Syria, Morocco, Yemen, Jordan, Saudi Arabia, Afghanistan, Pakistan, and Chechnya), has been deadly, troubling, and costly.[15] According to British officials, as reported in the *London Times*: "These are not just zealots who grabbed a gun and went to the front line. They know how to employ guerrilla tactics so someone had to have trained them. They are certainly organized, and if it's not bin Laden's people, it's al-Qaeda by another name. But they certainly came here to fight the West."[16] Therefore, the present conflict must be seen, as it is by al-Qaeda and other radical fundamentalist Muslim nations and organizations, as the global, total war they believe it to be—that is, World War IV.

This was hinted at by Andrew Sullivan as early as October 7th, 2001 when, writing in the *New York Times Magazine* under the title, "This *Is* a Religious War," he said:

> This coming conflict is indeed as momentous and as grave as the last major conflicts, against Nazism and Communism, and it is not hyperbole to see it in these epic terms. What is at stake is yet another battle against a religion that is succumbing to the temptation Jesus refused in the desert—to rule by force. The difference is that this conflict is against a more formidable enemy than Nazism or Communism. The secular totalitarianisms of the 20th century were, in

---

[15] Some 2000-plus deaths at this writing (early 2006).
[16] Reported in Yossef Bodansky, *The Secret History of the Iraq War*, 2004, p. 278.

President Bush's memorable words, "discarded lies." They were fundamentalisms built on the very weak intellectual conceits of a master race and a Communist revolution. But Islamic fundamentalism is based on a glorious civilization and a great faith. It can harness and co-opt and corrupt true and good believers if it has a propitious and toxic enough environment.[17]

In a videotaped message shortly after the 9/11 attacks, Osama bin Laden claimed that God Almighty himself had struck America through a group of "vanguard Muslims." The end is clear, he thundered: to destroy America.[18]

As Norman Podhoretz said in an article in *Commentary* Magazine:

This new enemy has already attacked us on our own soil—a feat neither Nazi Germany nor Soviet Russia ever managed to pull off—and openly announces his intention to hit us again, only this time with weapons of infinitely greater and deadlier power than those used on 9/11. His objective is not merely to murder as many of us as possible and to conquer our land. Like the Nazis and Communists before him, he is dedicated to the destruction of everything good for which America stands. It is this, then, that we...have a responsibility to uphold and are privileged to defend.[19]

As I've already said, the first front in the War on Terror, the military campaign against al-Qaeda and the Taliban regime that provided it with "aid and safe haven," met relatively little opposition either here at home or abroad. This was because it was easily justified as a retaliatory strike against the terrorists who had attacked us, and there was, in turn, very little sympathy for the Taliban. Yes, within weeks, observers, like R.W. Apple of the *New York Times,* rushed to conjure up the "ghost of Vietnam," arguing we

---

[17] Pages 44-57.

[18] Reported in Elsthain, *op. cit.*, pp. 85-86.

[19] "World War IV: How It Started, What It Means, And Why We Have to Win," September 2004.

were once again being sucked into a "quagmire." Well, it didn't happen, much to the chagrin of these critics. The terrifying psychological effect of 15,000-pound "Daisy Cutter" bombs that exploded just above the ground, wiping out everything for hundreds of yards, and the incredible precision of "smart-bomb" technology that was directed by "spotters" on the ground equipped with radios, laptops, and lasers, produced a devastating blow to a much-touted, battled-hardened enemy, while producing very few civilian casualties.

Unfortunately, Osama bin Laden was not captured and al-Qaeda was not totally destroyed, but it was dealt a devastating blow by the campaign in Afghanistan. Furthermore, on October 9th, 2004, despite inclement weather (two inches of snow in some places) and threats of spectacular attacks by terrorist insurgents, millions of Afghanis turned out to vote for a president in their first taste of democracy. According to the *Army News Service*, a woman from the village of Raban said: "The Taliban burned my house, they kicked us out of [town]. Now I have freedom. I'm standing in front of you and voting. Of course my life has been changed."[20] To me, this sounds like success, and it sends a strong message to countries that give safe haven to terrorists and, when given the chance, refuse to clean them out, that they are asking to be overthrown in favor of new leaders with democratic aspirations. The Afghan campaign proved that, instead of only being able to react in the law-enforcement mode that had proved so ineffective prior to 9/11, the military option was open, available for use, and lethally effective.

In his September 20th, 2001 speech, President Bush had said, "We will pursue nations that provide aid or safe haven to terrorism." But in his *State of the Union* speech on January 29th, 2002, he was even more explicit:

---

[20] Master Sgt. Terry Anderson, "Millions Vote in Afghan Elections," October 12, 2004.

> We'll be deliberate, yet time is not on our side. I will not wait on events, while dangers gather. I will not stand by, as peril draws closer and closer. The United States of America will not permit the world's most dangerous regimes to threaten us with the world's most destructive weapons.

Upon hearing this, it should have been clear to anyone that Mr. Bush, as Commander-in-Chief of the U.S. Armed Forces, was not willing to just sit around waiting for another 9/11 strike. Instead, he was now willing to take preemptive action. Although this was a logical extension of what he had said earlier, it went largely unnoticed until his June 1st, 2002 speech to the graduating class at West Point, when he placed his right to preemption in historical context:

> For much of the last century, America's defense relied on the cold-war doctrine of deterrence and containment. In some cases, those strategies still apply. But new threats also require new thinking. Deterrence—the promise of massive retaliation against nations—means nothing against shadowy terrorist networks with no nation or citizens to defend.

Although this covered al-Qaeda and other such groups, he then went on to explain why the old doctrines could not work with Saddam's regime in Iraq: "Containment is not possible when unbalanced dictators with weapons of mass destruction can deliver those weapons or missiles or secretly provide them to terrorist allies." He went on to say: "We cannot defend our friends by hoping for the best. We cannot put our faith in tyrants, who solemnly sign nonproliferation treaties, and then systematically break them." He then concluded:

> If we wait for threats to fully materialize, we will have waited too long.... [T]he war on terror will not be won on the defensive. We must take the battle to the enemy, disrupt his plans, and confront the worst threats before they emerge. In the world we have entered, the only path to safety is the path of action. And this nation will act.

Officially, the Bush administration was denying that it had reached any definite decision about what to do with Saddam Hussein, but everyone seemed to know that, in promising to act, he was zeroing in on him. Unlike Afghanistan, the thought of invading Iraq and overthrowing Saddam Hussein provoked a firestorm. It was immediately argued that the whole idea of preemptive action by the U.S. was not just a dangerous precedent, but was a violation of international law.

Now, if 9/11 changed the paradigm for post-Cold War international relations, as President Bush claimed, and I believe it did, then it was no longer prudent or morally defensible to simply sit back and wait for threats to fully develop, when such threats involved the potential loss of massive numbers of innocent civilians. Historically, there is nothing new about preemption. The President was simply drawing on nearly two hundred years of national history over the course of which preemption was both advocated and implemented. As Jean Bethke Elshtain pointed out in her excellent book *Just War Against Terror: The Burden of American Power in a Violent World*:

> The cries that preemption is something brand-new and a radical departure from the past do not bear up under close scrutiny. That does not make preemption right, of course, or justifiable by definition. But preempting horrific possibilities is very much in the air these days in debates among international relations and international law experts.[21]

She went on to say:

> What the just war tradition insists upon is that when states act, they do so under the rubric of just war requirements. In this way, argue just war thinkers, states are obligated to conduct their affairs with restraint, to justify themselves within a framework of ethical

---

[21] Page 191.

criteria, and to use those criteria as ongoing evaluative tools for their own activities.[22]

Now, having spent some time looking at history and philosophy, I realize I haven't yet set forth the reasons why I believe the Iraq War was just. My efforts so far have been to show that (1) the Iraq War—although a real war (and by this I mean a traditional war fought by national entities)—needs to be seen as a subset of the larger global War on Terror, (2) the Iraq War was a war that was won by Coalition Forces, and (3) we ought to see the post-war terrorist activities in Iraq as not simply an extension of a regional conflict, but as a continuation of the greater, global War on Terror—World War IV, if you will. With this said, let's turn our attention to a justification of the Iraq War.

In order to be just, under the *jus ad bellum* criteria of just war theory:

- A war must be a response to an act of aggression or the threat of such.

- A war must be openly declared.

- A war must begin with the right intentions—intentions that desire a more just, hence peaceful, world.

- A war should be a last resort after other options have been considered seriously. Other measures do not need to have been tried, in turn, but they must have been considered.

Notice, if you will, that these criteria *assume* that the state is the decision-making entity. This is important because so many opponents of the Iraq War have argued that "only" the UN, or a collectivity of some sort that included the French and Germans, could "legitimately" declare war. Such thinking is one-world-ism gone to seed and violates the principles of international law. It even contradicts the UN Charter, which presumes that its

---

[22] *Ibid.*

members are sovereign entities that have the right to defend themselves, and this means they have the right to determine in what that defense consists. Some may wish to disagree, but to claim that a state acting alone has no right to do so (the word being thrown around a lot today is "unilateralism"), is to deny the very right of the state to exist at all, and is just plain silliness. So, the idea that the United States acted illegally by invading Iraq because it did not have UN approval to do so does not comport with either the sovereign rights of states or the precepts of international law.

Therefore, President Bush, as Commander-in-Chief of the armed forces of the United States of America, had the right—when failing to secure UN approval and believing Saddam's regime a real and present danger to the security of the United States and its allies—to direct an invasion of Iraq. He made it clear from the very beginning of the conflict that our fight was not with the Iraqi people, but with the regime of a murderous tyrant who needed to be removed from power for the benefit of all nations of goodwill and the Iraqi people themselves. However, it is precisely at this point—namely, whether or not Saddam's regime really posed a preeminent threat—that we find the most controversy.

As we've now been told, there were no weapons of mass destruction (WMD) in Iraq, and there was absolutely no connection between Saddam's regime and al-Qaeda or other terrorist organizations. Because this misinformation is widely believed by many, it is time to examine these claims.

With reference to WMD and the Saddam Hussein-Osama bin Laden connection, there was universal agreement prior to the Iraq War that Saddam's regime had WMD and it was further known in intelligence circles that there had been ongoing cooperation between Saddam's intelligence services and bin Laden's terrorists since the early 1990s, when the jihadist forces in Somalia, under the command of Ayman al-Zawahiri, received extensive military assistance from the Iraqis via Sudan.[23] Mr. Bodansky, who was director of the Congressional Task Force on Terrorism and Unconventional Warfare for more than a decade, longtime director of research at the International Strategic Studies Association, and senior editor for the Defense and Foreign Affairs group of publications, has impeccable intelligence *bona fides*. He is not a Bushite, by any means, and has been critical of the Bush Administration's handling of the Iraq War, nevertheless, has written:

> The [Saddam-bin Laden] alliance was solidified in 1998-99, as Saddam and bin Laden realized that they needed each other's resources in order to confront the United States. Moreover, Iraq (working in conjunction with Yasser Arafat) had resolved to throw the Middle East into chaos—a move that threatened to imperil vital interests of America and its allies. The war Saddam Hussein contemplated, which included the use of weapons of mass destruction, would have caused inestimable damage to the global economy by disrupting energy supplies from the Persian Gulf.[24]

He went on to say:

> In the fall of 2002 Iraq crossed an unacceptable threshold, supplying operational weapons of mass destruction (WMD) to bin Laden's terrorists. These developments were confirmed to the Western intelligence services after several terrorists—graduates of WMD training programs—were captured in Israel, Chechnya, Turkey, and France, along with documents related to their activities. On the basis of pure threat analysis, the United States should have gone to war against Iraq, as well as its partners Syria and Iran, in fall 2002. By then there was already unambiguous evidence indicating the urgency of defusing the imminent danger posed by Iraq and its primary allies in the growing terrorist conspiracy.

---

[23] See Yossef Bodansky, *The Secret History of the Iraq War*, 2004, p. 1.
[24] *Ibid.*

And:

> As mighty as it is, however, America does not exist in a vacuum. Not without reason, the Bush administration elected to first attempt to build wider support for an American-led war, and undertaking that pushed the opening hostilities to spring 2003.[25]

I'll have more to say of the specific situation which Bodansky mentioned in a moment. But before doing so, it needs to be pointed out that in April, 2003, al-Qaeda's Center for Islamic Studies published a propaganda piece, entitled "The Crusaders' War Against Iraq," which stressed the Islamist role in Iraq. It argued that the American war against Iraq was but one facet of the fateful confrontation between Islam and the United States, and regardless of the outcome of the battle for Baghdad, "the battle is going to take place in various stages, and the stage we believe will exhaust the enemy has not come yet." "Therefore," the study went on to say, "we need to think practically about the way we can join the battle and support the Iraqi resistance force, which has so far exhibited enormous resistance, causing shock, fear, and confusion among the enemy." "The Nation's duty today," *and they are here speaking of all Muslims*, "is to maintain the state of shock and fear among the enemy that has invaded Muslim countries."[26]

About the same time, Thabit bin Qays, who was al-Qaeda's new media coordinator, elaborated on the subject in an e-mail addressed to the Saudi-owned, London-based magazine *al-Majallah*. In it, Thabit said "al-Qaeda's command is watching closely the events in Iraq as they unfold."[27] In fact, he acknowledged that al-Qaeda was *already* involved in the war: "Our activities are connected with the events in Iraq," but all further details were "a matter concerning the leader of al-Qaeda, Sheikh Osama bin Laden, [and] will be announced when the right time comes." A short time later, an audio tape from bin Laden surfaced in

---

[25] Bodansky, pp. 1-2.
[26] Bodansky, pp. 276-277.
[27] Bodansky, p.277.

Pakistan on which he said, "The United States has attacked Iraq, and soon it will also attack Iran, Saudi Arabia, Egypt, and Sudan." In response to that danger, he called upon Muslims everywhere to wage a total war against the United States.[28] He reserved his highest praise for suicide attackers: "I am proud of those martyrs who sacrificed their lives for the sake of Islam," adding that their primary contribution was in setting an example for a new generation of Muslims to emulate.

Now, let's turn our attention to the *casus belli* (or reason for war) of which Bodansky wrote in his extraordinary book. Most of you will recall from news reports that on January 14th, 2003, British police and security forces raided a terrorist safe house in Manchester, England in which a quantity of ricin, an extremely potent poison, was found. During the raid, a Scotland Yard detective was killed. Bodansky reveals that the investigation that brought about this raid had begun in Israel in the fall of 2002 and involved, at its peak, the intelligence services of more than six countries.[29] "The investigators' findings," according to Bodansky, "provided the 'smoking gun' supporting the administration's insistence on Iraq's centrality to global terrorism, the availability of operational weapons of mass destruction in Iraq, and proof of the close cooperation between Iraqi military intelligence and al-Qaeda."[30]

However, instead of using the data accumulated during the ensuing investigation to put to rest the mounting international criticism and skepticism in the media, the Bush administration decided to accommodate Prime Minister Tony Blair's strong pressure to keep Israel at arms' length, not to expose the complicity of Yassar Arafat and the Palestinian Authority that had been exposed during the investigation, and placate Blair's fellow West European leaders. Consequently, the American public was not presented with one of the strongest and clearest justifications for war with Iraq.

---

[28] *Ibid.*

[29] See the chapter in Bodansky's book entitled "Casus Belli," pp. 51-84.

[30] Page 51.

It all started when Israeli Special Forces, on the night of September 13th, 2002, captured a three-man squad attempting to cross the Jordan River and enter the Palestinian territories on their way to Arafat's compound in Ramallah. Their subsequent interrogations—and the Israelis are well-known for successes in this area—revealed they were highly trained members of the Baghdad-based Arab Liberation Front (ALF) and that they had been sent to conduct spectacular strikes under the banner of Arafat's Fatah ("Fatah" is a reverse acronym of the Arabic *Harekat at-Tahrir al-Wataniyyeh al-Falastiniyyeh*, and means "conquest by means of jihad"). The ALF, although not a well-publicized organization, is a vehicle through which Saddam's regime has distributed millions of dollars to the families of Palestinian suicide bombers or "martyrs," as they are called by the Islamists. Specifically, they had been dispatched by ALF Chief Muhammad Zaidan Abbas (aka, Abu-al-Abbas) to operate directly under the control of Tawfiq Tirawi, chief of the Palestinian Authority's General Intelligence Service, and Arafat's closest confidant. Abbas and Tirawi were very close childhood friends, having grown up together in a village just north of Ramallah, where they eventually joined Arafat's fledgling terrorist organization, al-Fatah, in the early 1960s.

The task of the three ALF terrorists, it was learned, was multi-operational, including using shoulder-fired missiles to shoot down civilian airlines as they took off from and approached Ben-Gurion Airport and using anti-tank rockets and missiles to ambush convoys, including American units on their way to Iraq. In addition, they were to organize and train Palestinian terrorists—all trusted operatives of Tirawi's—to assist in operations and intelligence gathering inside Israel. They said that when they had been briefed in Baghdad, they were told they would receive all the equipment and weapons they needed from al-Fatah via Tirawi.

During the previous summer, they said, they had received, along with other squads of ALF terrorists, special training at Salman Pak—a highly secret terrorist training facility southeast of Baghdad where both Iraqis and non-Iraqi Arabs received training on hijacking planes and trains, planting explosives in cities, sabotage, and assassinations—by the infamous Unit 999, an ultra-secret Iraqi special forces "deep penetration" unit that was tasked by Saddam with both domestic and foreign operations, and was part of the *Al-Istikhbarat al-Askariyya* (Special Branch of Iraqi Military Intelligence). They recounted that in an adjacent part of the camp, other teams of Unit 999 were training a select group of terrorists specifically identified as members of al-Qaeda. Although their training was separate, and those involved used code names, they were able to learn a lot about the missions of their Islamist cohorts. The three ALF terrorists told the Israelis that their jihadi colleagues received elaborate training in chemical weapons and poisons, especially ricin. As they moved to deploy, they were moved into areas under the control of Ansar-al-Islam, Osama bin Laden's Kurdish offshoot. There they experimented with chemical weapons and poisons. From there, the ALF said, the jihadis traveled to Turkey, where they were to strike American bases with chemical weapons once the war started, and to Pakinsy Gore in northern Georgia (on the border with Chechnya) to aid Chechen terrorists as they launched major terrorist operations against Russia. Others were dispatched to train jihadi teams arriving from Western Europe via Turkey in sophisticated terrorism techniques, including the use of chemical weapons and ricin.

Soon there was independent confirmation of the information being provided by the ALF terrorists. Turkish security forces, acting on tips from the Israelis, arrested two al-Qaeda operatives poring over plans to attack the U.S. airbase at Incerlick with chemical weapons, and American intelligence also learned from their own independent sources about the activities of foreign mujahedin in Georgia's Pakinsy Gore. Then, and who can forget it, on October 23rd, a group of Chechen and Arab terrorists captured a Moscow theater in the middle of a performance. In the process, they took over seven hundred people hostage, rigging the theater with bombs and threatening to kill everyone in the building. When negotiations failed and the terrorists shot at least one of the hostages to demonstrate their determination, Russian anti-terrorist forces broke into the theater after using a special knockout gas to neutralize the Chechens before they were able to detonate their bombs, which was considered to be the salvation of most of the hostages. Nevertheless, almost two hundred hostages died from the secondary effects of the gas, including heart attacks and choking on their own vomit. However, the mere occurrence of a spectacular strike in Moscow meant that there could no longer be any doubt about the accuracy of the information provided by the three Palestinians in Israel's custody.

Even so, the White House was still reluctant to advertise what they knew because it would expose Israeli involvement, and it was trying to do everything it could to keep the Israelis out of the War on Terror for fear it would deter the participation of Arab and Muslim countries in the forming coalition. Even so, Israel was quitly sharing the acquired data with several European governments, leading to the eventual disruption and capture of several Arab and Chechen terrorist networks in Paris, London, and Manchester, as well as related support networks in Spain and Italy. Chemical weapons and ricin had played important roles in the disruption of all these networks, which had, in turn, been trained in Georgia's Pakinsy Gore. And so when ricin was discovered in the Manchester raid, all the dots connected and the Israeli intelligence was proven totally correct. Consequently, on the eve of war with Iraq, the intelligence services of the Western European governments knew that Saddam Hussein's regime needed to be toppled, and that it needed to be done sooner rather than later.

Even so, most Western European governments, for a variety of reasons (some of which involved their own complicity) staunchly refused to address Iraqi training of al-Qaeda terrorists in the use of chemical weapons and poisons. Further, the public acknowledgment of this evidence would have exposed the intimate involvement of Yasser Arafat and the Palestinian Authority in international terrorism, something they did not want to do for political and other nefarious reasons. Moreover, in the winter of 2002, Tony Blair led the European effort to salvage Arafat, actually rewarded him with a Palestinian state in hopes of demonstrating that the War on Terror was not indiscriminately anti-Arab or anti-Muslim. The rest is history, as they say. Having to choose between further alienating the Western Europeans, who were insistent in keeping Arafat out of it, and bolstering its case against Iraq by providing the concrete Israeli evidence, Mr. Bush, in what I consider to be a serious misstep, decided to go with the Europeans.

So, on February 5th, 2003, Secretary of State Colin Powell, in his speech to the UN, showed an aerial shot of the Ansar-al-Islam facility, which he identified as a "poison and explosive training center." When foreign media pointed out the derelict status of the facility, Washington remained silent rather than hint at evidence that would confirm Powell's claim but also prove Arafat's involvement in Iraqi terrorism and WMD, and that would have pointed directly to Israel's contribution to the effort to disarm Iraq.

Does this mean that I believe the President "lied" about his reason for toppling Saddam Hussein? No, it doesn't. On the contrary, he had every reason to believe Saddam's regime was a clear and present danger to America and its allies. What it means, though, is that the President of the United States made a decision, based upon the various reasons that had been presented to him, that I do not think was best for the country. Have I lost faith in him? Certainly not! From my own mistakes, I know hindsight is much better than foresight. Furthermore, I cannot imagine anyone who could have done much better than Mr. Bush at a time so critical in our history. On the other hand, I can think of more than a few who I believe would have done much worse, including Al Gore, who seems to be clueless even about the events that happened and decisions that were made during the eight years of the Clinton administration—events and decisions of which he was supposed to have been a key player.

Add to these events one of the most divisive presidential campaigns in recent history, and you have a potent formula for the political trash and rhetorical garbage that has plagued the Bush administration's efforts to prosecute the War on Terror, especially the campaign to oust Saddam and its aftermath. What the Democratic hopefuls in this presidential campaign have done in their criticism of this administration's post-9/11 performance is absolutely shameful, and I think in some cases even treasonous.[31] Furthermore, the mainstream media has once again played the

---

[31] The only exception was Senator Joe Lieberman, who although I disagree with many of his political positions, nevertheless, proved himself a true patriot by not politicizing the war.

anti-war card it played during the Vietnam War. In the late 1960s, public opinion continued to support the Vietnam War, but unfortunately public opinion had ceased to count. In fact, as the *Tet* offensive of 1968 proved, even reality itself ceased to count, for all eventually came to agree that *Tet* was a crushing defeat for the North Vietnamese. Yet, all Walter Cronkite had to do from his anchor desk at CBS *Evening News* was to declare it a defeat for American forces, and a defeat it became. Likewise, all the mainstream media have had to do today is declare, without doing the painstaking research and intelligence gathering they have done in so many other investigations and exposés, that the al-Qaeda-Iraq connection was nothing but a fabrication concocted by the Bush administration in order to justify the President's long-standing vendetta against Saddam Hussein—a grudge that went back to Saddam's involvement in the thwarted 1993 assassination attempt against Bush Sr., who had led the Desert-Storm coalition that drove Saddam's forces out of Kuwait in 1991. Add to this the media attention given to trumped-up charges Michael Moore makes in his "Fahrenheit 9/11," and many Americans now believe the President, along with his cabinet, totally fabricated the al-Qaeda-Iraq connection *and* the issue of WMD. On October 7th, 2004, just twenty-six days before the Presidential Election, John Kerry brazenly proclaims that the Bush administration totally "fictionalized" the threat from Saddam Hussein.[32] This matched what his wife had said a little earlier: "Iraq and terrorism had nothing to do with one another. Zero."

Oh, really? Why then had Iraq been on the State Department's list of state sponsors of terror for more than a decade, most of which, not incidentally, was under President Bill Clinton? Why did the bipartisan Senate Intelligence Committee Report—a report panel member John Edwards approved—confirm this state sponsorship?

---

[32] Stephen F. Hayes, "Remember October 7th," *The Weekly Standard*, October 8, 2004.

Then there was the October 27th, 2003 memo sent from Undersecretary of Defense for Policy, Douglas J. Feith, to Senators Pat Roberts and Jay Rockefeller, the chairman and vice chairman of the Senate Intelligence Committee. According to Stephen F. Hayes, who referred to the classified memo in *The Weekly Standard*:

It was written in response to a request from the committee as a part of its investigation into prewar intelligence claims made by the administration. Intelligence reporting in the 16-page memo comes from a variety of domestic and foreign agencies, including the FBI, the Defense Intelligence Agency, the Central Intelligence Agency, and the National Security Agency. Much of the evidence is detailed, conclusive, and corroborated by multiple sources. Some of it is new information obtained in custodial interviews with high-level al Qaeda terrorists and Iraqi officials, and some of it more than a decade old. The picture that emerges is one of a history of collaboration between two of America's most determined and dangerous enemies.[33]

He went on to say:

According to the memo—which lays out the intelligence in 50 numbered points—Iraq-al Qaeda contacts began in 1990 and continued through mid-March 2003, days before the Iraq War began. Most of the numbered passages contain straight, fact-based intelligence reporting, which in some cases includes an evaluation of the credibility of the source. The reporting is often followed by commentary and analysis.

Anyone interested in pursuing this further should get a copy of Hayes' article in *The Weekly Standard*, but suffice it to say that there is a preponderance of evidence that there was, in fact, an

---

[33] "Case Closed: The U.S. government's secret memo detailing cooperation between Saddam Hussein and Osama bin Laden," *The Weekly Standard*, November 24, 2003.

Osama bin Laden-Saddam Hussein connection *before,* *during* and *after* the Iraq War. (Incidentally, it was reported in the January 27th, 2004 issue of the Washington Post, that "Vice President Cheney...in an interview this month with the Rocky Mountain News, recommended as the 'best source of information' an article in *The Weekly Standard* magazine detailing a relationship between Hussein and al Qaeda based on leaked classified information.")

Let's now turn our attention to WMD. When the Duelfer Report was released to the public on October 7th, 2004, "Gotcha, Mr. President" was the consensus headline in nearly every daily newspaper in America the next day. This report, prepared by Charles A. Duelfer, relays the findings of the Special Advisor to the Director of Central Intelligence on Iraq's Weapons of Mass Destruction. Sadly, the report confirmed what most of us had already come to expect after months and months of fruitless searching by a thousand-plus inspectors: there has not been found any stockpiles of weapons of mass destruction in Iraq since the war began in March, 2003. It also concluded that whatever illicit weapons Saddam Hussein did possess were most likely destroyed just after the 1991 Gulf War in accordance with U.N. sanctions. However, what failed to be reported by most of those same newspapers was the findings that the report highlighted in the first line of its Key Findings summary:

Key Findings

Saddam Husayn so dominated the Iraqi Regime that its strategic intent was his alone. He wanted to end sanctions while preserving the capability to reconstitute his weapons of mass destruction (WMD) when sanctions were lifted.

• Saddam totally dominated the Regime's strategic decision making. He initiated most of the strategic thinking upon which decisions were made, whether in matters of war and peace (such as invading Kuwait), maintaining WMD as a national strategic goal, or on how Iraq was to position itself in the international community. Loyal dissent was discouraged and constructive variations to the implementation of his wishes on strategic issues were rare. Saddam was the Regime in a strategic sense and his intent became Iraq's strategic policy.

• Saddam's primary goal from 1991 to 2003 was to have UN sanctions lifted, while maintaining the security of the Regime. He sought to balance the need to cooperate with UN inspections—to gain support for lifting sanctions—with his intention to preserve Iraq's intellectual capital for WMD with a minimum of foreign intrusiveness and loss of face. Indeed, this remained the goal to the end of the Regime, as the starting of any WMD program, conspicuous or otherwise, risked undoing the progress achieved in eroding sanctions and jeopardizing a political end to the embargo and international monitoring.

• The introduction of the Oil-For-Food program (OFF) in late 1996 was a key turning point for the Regime. OFF rescued Baghdad's economy from a terminal decline created by sanctions. The Regime quickly came to see that OFF could be corrupted to acquire foreign exchange both to further undermine sanctions and to provide the means to enhance dual-use infrastructure and potential WMD-related development.

• By 2000-2001, Saddam had managed to mitigate many of the effects of sanctions and undermine their international support. Iraq was within striking distance of a de facto end to the sanctions regime, both in terms of oil exports and the trade embargo, by the end of 1999.

Saddam wanted to recreate Iraq's WMD capability—which was essentially destroyed in 1991—after sanctions were removed and Iraq's economy stabilized, but probably with a different mix of capabilities to that which previously existed. Saddam aspired to develop a nuclear capability—in an incremental fashion, irrespective of international pressure and the resulting economic risks—but he intended to focus on ballistic missile and tactical chemical warfare (CW) capabilities.

• Iran was the pre-eminent motivator of this policy. All senior level Iraqi officials considered Iran to be Iraq's principal enemy in the region. The wish to balance Israel and acquire status and influence in the Arab world were also considerations, but secondary.

• Iraq Survey Group (ISG) judges that events in the 1980s and early 1990s shaped Saddam's belief in the value of WMD. In Saddam's view, WMD helped to save the Regime multiple times. He believed that during the Iran-Iraq war chemical weapons had halted Iranian ground offensives and that ballistic missile attacks on Tehran had broken its political will. Similarly, during Desert Storm, Saddam believed WMD had deterred Coalition Forces from pressing their attack beyond the goal of freeing Kuwait. WMD had even played a role in crushing the Shi'a revolt in the south following the 1991 cease-fire.

• The former Regime had no formal written strategy or plan for the revival of WMD after sanctions. Neither was there an identifiable group of WMD policy makers or planners separate from Saddam. Instead, his lieutenants understood WMD revival was his goal from their long association with Saddam and his infrequent, but firm, verbal comments and directions to them.

Sort of paints a different picture of Saddam than many would have us to believe, doesn't it?

Truth is, Saddam sealed his own fate by supporting and exporting terror, and by failing to cooperate with the international inspections that were originally designed to force him to verify his disarmament—a role Senator Kerry and others seem not to have the slightest understanding of. The on-again/off-again inspection regime established by the U.N. Security Council in the wake of the Gulf War was never about a certain number of inspections, or even whether the U.N. inspectors could independently verify the status of Saddam's weapons programs. It was, instead, about verifying that Saddam Hussein actively engaged in disarmament and, in turn, his providing *positive evidence* of that disarmament. Given Saddam's proclivity for successfully hiding his illicit weapons activities in a country about the size of California, there could be no assurance he had disarmed unless and until he cooperated in fully documenting his disarmament. As Clinton's Defense Secretary, William Cohen, put it in November of 1998:

[Inspectors] have to find documents, computer discs, production points, ammunition areas in an area that size. Hussein has said, "We have no programs now." We're saying, "Prove it." He says he has destroyed all his nerve agent. [W]e're asking "where, when and how?"... The onus for this is firmly on Saddam Hussein.

Even former President Clinton has made it clear that "it is incontestable that on the day I left office [in January 2001], there were unaccounted for stocks of biological and chemical weapons [in Iraq]." And even Hans Blix, on January 27th, 2003, informed the U.N. Security Council that "...Iraq appears not to have come to a genuine acceptance—not even today—of the disarmament, which was demanded of it and which it needs to carry out to win the confidence of the world and to live in peace." He went on, in that same report, to say that the "hide and seek" methods employed by the Iraqis forced the inspectors to try and map the weapons programs and to search for evidence through inspections, interviews, seminars, inquiries with suppliers and intelligence organizations. On February 14th, 2003, Blix told the Security Council that:

> If Iraq had provided the necessary cooperation in 1991, the phase of disarmament—under resolution 687 (1991)—could have been short and a decade of sanctions could have been avoided. Today, three months after the adoption of resolution 1441 (2002), the period of disarmament through inspection could still be short, if "immediate, active and unconditional cooperation" with UNMOVIC and the IAEA were to be forthcoming.

So, with Saddam Hussein purposefully failing to verify the dismantling of his WMD, how was anyone able to believe he didn't still have them? In fact, in April, 2003, former Secretary Cohen flatly stated that:

> I am convinced that [Saddam] has them. I saw evidence back in 1998 when we would see the inspectors being barred from gaining entry into a warehouse for three hours with trucks rolling up and then moving those trucks out. I am absolutely convinced that there are weapons. We will find them.

In fact, it wasn't very long ago that John Kerry, John Edwards, and even French Foreign Minister Dominique de Villepin were talking about Iraq's WMD with much the same certitude as Condoleezza Rice, Dick Cheney, and Donald Rumsfeld.

So, prior to and during the Iraq War, there was every reason to believe that WMD remained stockpiled in Iraq, that it held large amounts of banned materials, and that it, in concert with other groups, sought to bypass WMD bans by attempting to develop effective ways to "weaponize" deadly nerve and biological agents, such as VX (a deadly nerve gas), anthrax, aflatoxin, and botulinum. These agents were known to have been produced (this is not speculation, in that Iraq itself admitted to producing them), and in significant amounts. It was the U.N. that discovered that Iraq had manufactured VX and was developing a biological warfare program. And all of this predates the Bush administration's cataloging of banned and suspected WMD. In other words, contrary to what some are claiming today, these were not just "lies" trumped up by the Bush administration in order to tout war with Iraq. If so, then what did Clinton's former Secretary of State Madeleine Albright, when ambassador to the U.N., mean when she said that Saddam's weapons program could "destroy all humanity"? Was she "lying" too?

In the "anti-knowledge" framework that so many seem to be operating in today, will the media now pick up on the claim by one prominent professor of religion that there was never any compelling evidence that Saddam actually gassed the Kurdish people in northern Iraq? In fact, the horrific attack has been documented by mountains of evidence and confirmed by an army of human rights activists, diplomats, journalists, aid workers, and survivors.

For those who have not fallen victim to the "anti-knowledge" cartel, the combination of a repressive regime, WMD, and international terrorism, and the ability of this triad to disturb the peace of the world, and in view of the frightful blow our enemies delivered to us on 9/11, and with the realization that President Bush was and is obviously privy to classified intelligence information that was not, and probably still hasn't been, made known to the public, and with the pressure on him as the head of a state with the means to do something about it, I am comfortable in thinking that President Bush, in seeing to it that Saddam's regime was removed from power, operated in a reasonable and prudent fashion to a clear and present danger. May God bless him as he rules justly and righteously is my prayer.

Was the Iraq War justified? Absolutely! Is the War on Terror that continues to be waged in Iraq and other places in the world just? Yes, as just as they come. Is it being conducted justly? Yes, it is—by our side, that is, not the terrorists. In fact, so far, it is the most justly fought war in history. This is a reflection of the fact that the U.S. Military, at this moment in time, organizes all of its training, strategy, and tactics with the just war theory of proportionality and discrimination in mind, and this means, above all else, doing one's utmost to distinguish between combatants and noncombatants. Furthermore, it's a shame that more people don't know that American soldiers are trained to refuse to obey illegal orders under the code of restraints called the "law of war," which are rules derived in large part from the historic development of the just war tradition and its spin-offs as set forth in international conventions and arrangements. Consequently, the bitter debate that will continue about the Iraq War and its aftermath will continue to zero in on whether there was a justifiable reason for the Iraq War. It is my hope this chapter will help the interested reader, who may not yet have his or her mind made up about the justification for the war, to finally make an informed decision.

With this said, one must keep in mind that war is not a perfect science. Mistakes are always made—some strategic, some moral—and the Iraq War and its aftermath is no different. But if the terrorist plague that now threatens the West is to be eradicated (or at least significantly diminished), then the jihadist swamps where such terror breeds will have to be drained. The war with Iraq was a means to that end. However, there are other swamps to be drained, and the task ahead will be daunting, even for the world's only remaining superpower. But with God's help, the long, arduous work ahead can be won, and what person in his right mind is there who would think that those of us in the West would be better off losing to the jihadists?

I would like to conclude with the words of Norman Podhoretz, who I cited earlier:

> Now "our entire security as a nation"—including, to a greater extent than in 1947, our physical security—once more depends on whether we are ready and willing to accept and act upon the

responsibilities of moral and political leadership that history has yet again so squarely placed upon our shoulders. Are we ready? Are we willing? I think we are, but the jury is still out, and will not return a final verdict until well after the election of 2004.

May God bless us all as we try to think biblically and logically about this subject, and may God continue to bless America, is my prayer.

Chapter 11

What About Capital Punishment?

C apital punishment is a controversial subject. It is the kind of subject that tends to polarize people. Either one is for it or against it; there just doesn't seem to be much middle ground on the subject. Back when I first started thinking about the article that now makes up this chapter, there were 1,289 individuals on death rows in thirty-four states.[1] At that time, the last man to have been executed was sixty-six year-old Anthony Antone, who was electrocuted in Florida. Antone, an Organized Crime figure, was convicted of the contract murder of Richard Cloud, a former working associate of mine. While Dick was a detective with the Tampa Police Department and I was a detective with the Hillsborough County Sheriff's Office, we worked on several cases together. I remember, fondly, a commendation I received from the Los Angeles Police Department that was the direct result of Dick's invaluable assistance on a very important investigation.[2]

Dick Cloud was the kind of policeman of which stories are written and movies are made. He was tenacious, unorthodox, implacable, and, unfortunately, very, very tough. (He was fired from the TPD for using "excessive force." Whether this charge was actually true, or the machinations of something much more sinister, I do not know with any certainty. Even so, Cloud was tough and it

---

[1] By 2005, the most recent year for which we have data, that rate had risen to 3,383.

[2] This was back when the LAPD was known as one of the finest police departments in the country.

could have been legitimate.) When Det. Cloud was assigned a case, he did not let up until the perpetrator was arrested, convicted, and serving time. Needless to say, he was the kind of policeman who made enemies. In fact, it seems he was always receiving death threats, and on several occasions it had even been rumored that certain individuals had put a contract out on him. Unfortunately, when Cloud was fired from the police department, he was no longer "protected." In other words, it is a well-known fact that gangsters do not usually kill police officers, because they do not want the entire law enforcement community breathing down their necks. But Anthony Antone, evidently thinking that Cloud was "safe," put a contract out on him and he was murdered as he answered a knock at the front door of his home. He was shot several times by a hit-man who posed as a door-to-door salesman. He left a wife and young son.

I found it extremely ironic that when Anthony Antone became, at that time, the twelfth person to be executed since 1976, his final statement to the press was, "Father, forgive them, for they know not what they do."

Furthermore, Willie Jasper Darden, an individual I arrested for murder back in the 70s, has subsequently been put to death in the Florida electric chair. Before finally dying, Darden's case went all the way to the U.S. Supreme Court. Why? The prosecutor at his trial had called him an "animal" and, therefore, he (Darden) did not feel he had received a fair trial. The Supreme Court ruled that he did, in fact, receive a fair trial in spite of the prosecutor's "error."

Although Darden was only charged and convicted for one murder, I am convinced, along with others, beyond any reasonable doubt, that he raped and murdered many women in the Tampa Bay area. Incidentally, when I arrested Darden he was actually serving time for rape! Yes, you read correctly. You see, the prison system was allowing this convicted felon to take weekend furloughs, and the findings of the subsequent investigation were that each time he was furloughed he raped and murdered someone else. Does this seem incredible to you? Well, wake up and take a real good look at the American Criminal Justice System, a system you erroneously think to be doing an adequate job of protecting you and your loved ones. Although our current subject matter does not allow me to do so, I could further relate real events about the Criminal Justice System that would send cold chills up and down your spine. Permit me to just say this: *I can assure you that after hearing these stories you would never again feel safe under our current system of criminal justice.*

This all, of course, creates strong emotional feelings for me, and I know that I have a great deal of passion concerning this issue. In fact, some of you may even think my personal involvement disqualifies me from dealing objectively with the issue of capital punishment. I pray this is not the case, and the only reason I have mentioned my personal involvement is to let you know that I have had to give this subject my serious attention over the years. If I have misunderstood what God has had to say on this subject, then I am wrong; and if I am wrong, then I need to repent. For me, the arguments for or against capital punishment are not part of some academic exercise to be conducted in an "ivory tower" somewhere. On the contrary, it is a serious question that affects me where I live.

It is my sincere belief that capital punishment is commanded, ordained, sanctified, and authorized by God's Word. It will be my responsibility in this chapter to demonstrate from the Bible the truth of this position. If I am unable to do so, then my thesis must be rejected by every lover of the truth. On the other hand, if my thesis is substantiated, then it must be received by all who would respect the Bible.

Although many seem to think this issue is purely political, it is clear to me that even when its political ramifications are understood, it must be seen, first and foremost, as a religious question, namely: *Is capital punishment moral or immoral?* In fact, much of the most excited, passionate, and vehement objections to the death penalty come from religious individuals who believe it to be contrary to God's will. It should be clear, then, that this is not some trivial issue. If as some are saying, God is against capital punishment, then the state has no right to exact the death penalty. Conversely, if capital punishment has been ordained by the Creator, then there can be no legitimate argument against it, so long as it is carried out under conditions consistent with justice and righteousness.

Having set the stage for this study, let us now turn our attention to the Word of God.

The Old Testament

It is only fitting that we begin this study at the beginning. In Genesis 9:6, God said, "Whoso sheddeth man's blood, by man shall his blood be shed: for in the image of God made He man." Although there are some who look upon this statement as utterly barbaric, most have recognized this principle as the foundation of civilized society. Man is unique in that he is made in the image of the Creator, and his "right to life" must not be interfered with by any other creature. If this principle or law is broken, and a man is murdered, then the murderer must be put to death.[3] This moral law stands apart from the Law of Moses given at Sinai, and has no more been rescinded than the fact that man is made in the image of God. (I'll have more to say about this later in the chapter.)

As Genesis 9:6 tells us, God has universally legislated against murder; therefore, it should not surprise us to see this principle incorporated into the Law of Moses. In Exodus 20:13, the Decalogue says, "Thou shall not kill." Consequently, it is, I think, a bit ironic that on those rare occasions when the death penalty is being administered today, we see protesters outside the prisons carrying signs that say, "THOU SHALL NOT KILL." I would to God that these misguided, sign-carrying, religious zealots, along with the liberal media, really did understand the meaning of God's prohibition against murder.

Exodus 20:13 was never written to be a prohibition of capital punishment, as the anti-capital punishment protesters imply. Instead, it was written as a prohibition against murder. This is made quite clear when one reads Exodus 21:12, which says, "He that smiteth a man, so that he die, shall be surely put to death."

---

[3] See Gen. 9:5-6.

Incidentally, under the Law of Moses, no substitute or alternative was accepted for the execution of a murderer. If the murderer was not executed, the land was defiled according to Numbers 35:30-33. Clearly, then, the God of the Old Testament not only believed in capital punishment, He demanded it!

The New Testament

Although God's attitude about capital punishment in the Old Testament cannot be misunderstood, some are convinced He changed His mind in the New Testament. According to some, capital punishment seems much too cruel a penalty to be condoned by the meek and humble Jesus. According to others, the God of the Old Testament was the product of a primitive people; therefore, He was represented as a vengeful and barbaric Deity. As we have become more "civilized," a more loving, caring, and forgiving Deity has been produced. According to these theologians, the God of the New Testament is the "mellowed-out" God of the Old Testament. (I mention this not because I think any sincere Bible student would believe it, but to emphasize how easy it is for men to profane the Almighty God and turn to idols. We must be content to let God be God. We must always be very careful that we are seeing Him as He has really revealed Himself. Otherwise, we just may be dabbling in idolatry.) The God of the Old Testament and the God of the New Testament are the same God. He has not changed in any of His characteristics or attributes.[4] Keeping this truth in mind will prevent us from making some serious mistakes about God's attitude about capital punishment today.

In Matthew 19:18, Jesus, who according to John 1:1-17 was God incarnate, said, "Thou shall do no murder." This, of course, proved what we should already intuitively know; namely, God's moral prohibition against murder has not changed. Murder has been, is, and always will be wrong, and the Bible accurately portrays it as such. As long as man is made in the image of God,

---

[4] See Mal. 3:6; Jas. 1:17.

murder will be wrong. Everyone, and especially those who claim to be following Jesus, should know that God's moral code forbids murder.[5] On this truth there should be no disagreement. Where disagreement does occur, however, is on the subject of whether or not the penalty for murder remains the same.

The Case Of The Adulterous Woman

John 8:1-11 has often been used to teach that under Christ the death penalty must no longer be enforced. Therefore, it would certainly be to our advantage to spend a little time studying the details of this case. Under the Law of Moses, adultery was a capital offense.[6] Those Scribes and Pharisees who, in John 8:5, brought the alleged adulterous woman to Jesus that day in the Jerusalem Temple understood this teaching, for they said, "Now Moses in the law commanded us, that such should be stoned: but what sayest thou?" But, and this has some bearing on the case, they were not the least bit interested in seeing justice done that day. If they were, where was the man she had been involved with? Under the Law of Moses, both the adulterer and the adulteress were to be stoned, and it must be remembered that this alleged adulteress had been caught "in the very act," according to verse 4. No, we can be sure that these men were not concerned with justice being done. Instead, they were, as verse 6 makes clear, hoping for some reason to accuse the Lord.

When Jesus finally answered, He said, "He that is without sin among you, let him first cast a stone at her." It ought to be obvious that when He made this statement He was not saying that the only way capital punishment could be meted out would be by those who had never sinned. Otherwise, how could anyone have ever carried out the commandment to execute murderers under the Law of Moses? It has been said, "That which proves too much, proves nothing." Staying within the context, then, it is apparent

---

[5] See Rom. 13:9; 1 Pet. 4:15; 1 Jn. 3:15.
[6] See Deut. 22:22.

Jesus was addressing Himself to the evil motives of these men, who were actually much more perverse than the woman they were accusing. Remember, this was mob action, and if Jesus would have given His consent to that mob, they were ready to stone the woman to death, which would have been contrary to Roman law, and then lay the whole blame at His feet. If, on the other hand, He said "No" to their intent to stone the woman, then they stood ready to accuse Him before the people as one who taught against the Law of Moses. These were vile men, indeed!

Moreover, and much more importantly, it must not be forgotten that this whole episode was actually taking place contrary to the Law of Moses. Under the Law of Moses, the accused had the right to a fair trial. But, as we have already pointed out, the men in this case were not really interested in justice. Nevertheless, Jesus conducted Himself wonderfully. Under the weight of their own sins, these men withdrew themselves and their charges against the accused. As a result, some have mistakenly thought that the Lord then had the right to stone her Himself, and because He did not do so proves that capital punishment, under the Law of Christ, is no longer right for adultery, as well as murder, rape, or any other offense specified in the Law of Moses. This is a serious mistake!

One must not lose sight of the fact that this whole scenario occurred under the Law of Moses. Under Moses' Law it took two or more witnesses before one could be sentenced to death, according to Deuteronomy 17:5-7. Jesus, who was, in fact, God in the flesh, was under obligation to keep the Law of Moses perfectly; therefore, He could not have stoned the woman Himself, or instructed anyone else to do so, without at least the two witnesses the Law required. Consequently, the woman in this case did not die because capital punishment was not justified for the offense of which she had been accused, as some are teaching, but because there was no one to accuse her. (Incidentally, if the *prima facie* case presented to Jesus had ever been officially heard before the Sanhedrin, she most assuredly would have been acquitted.) To read into this passage an anti-capital punishment position on the part of Jesus is to do violence to God's Word, and leads one to miss the whole point of this passage: It was the accusers, not the alleged adulterous woman, on trial that day. In other words, the lesson the Lord taught that day in the Temple concerned itself with the perversity of a religious people who had become worse than those they condemned. This, of course, is a lesson for all of us to take to heart.

The Apostle Paul's Position

When Paul was on trial before Festus, he stated, "For if I be an offender, or have committed anything worthy of death, I refuse not to die: but if there be none of these things whereof these accuse me, no man may deliver me unto them."[7] Paul's argument is that capital punishment is appropriate for certain offenses ("I refuse not to die"), but if no one could convict him of any of these offenses, then he should not be turned over to the Jews, who planned to kill him. Those who insist the death penalty is prohibited by the teachings of the New Testament find themselves arguing against the apostle Paul who, it must not be forgotten, was inspired by the Holy Spirit.

Romans Thirteen

Christianity was not designed as a blueprint for theocratic government. The Everlasting Kingdom knows no city, county, state, or national boundaries. Therefore, God ordained civil government to carry out punishment against evildoers.[8] The Kingdom of God (the church of Jesus Christ) and the kingdom of men (the civil government as recognized by its citizens and foreign powers) are clearly not the same, but each co-exists on this earthly plane with the other. This is not, as some have erroneously supposed, with one kingdom being good and the other evil; but, both are good, existing for different purposes: one spiritual, the other temporal. Civil government, as identified in Romans 13:1-7, is ordained by

---

[7] Acts 25:11.
[8] See Rom. 13:1-7; I Pet. 2:13,14.

God as a mechanical remedy against evil, so as to make life in this physical world somewhat more tolerable.

In Romans 13:4, Paul says that civil rulers "beareth not the sword in vain." Most of the expositors agree that this phrase does not mean only the "symbol of authority, but the actual sword in the hands of the executioner who inflicts the death penalty on criminals."[9]

Romans 13:1-7 clearly teaches that capital punishment is still ordained of God, is a terror, and, as such, should be feared. Of course, capital punishment must always be carried out by the state in a way consistent with righteousness and justice.[10] The death penalty must always be carried out in keeping with due process in conjunction with competent, lawfully constituted authority. If civil government administers capital punishment in such a way as to become a terror to law-abiding citizens, then it would need to be condemned.

The Murderer Is A Despiser Of Both God And Man

In his highly informative book, *Christian Ethics in Secular Society*, Philip E. Hughes wrote: "The preciousness of human life is evident in the requirement not only that an animal which causes a man's death (and thereby overturns the proper order of creation) should be deprived of life, but also that the man who murders his brother is to be put to death, because in doing so he has despised the image of God with which his being is imprinted and has treated his fellow man as though he were a brute beast whose life can be taken without compunction." This, I believe, is an accurate exposition of Genesis 9:5-6. When the death penalty is not imposed for murder, the unique and inviolable character of man is, in effect, denied; murder is, then, equivalent to lesser crimes, and the life of man is cheapened; but, even more importantly, the Creator is despised and profaned. Governments, then, in order to

---

[9] R.C.H Lenski, *St. Paul's Epistle To The Romans*, p. 792.

[10] See II Sam. 23:3; Ezek. 45:9; Dan. 4:25b-27.

be pleasing to God, must view the life of every human being as sacrosanct, and protect it with the ultimate penalty a temporal tribunal may inflict: capital punishment.

Conclusion

All who honestly consider the question of capital punishment must move beyond the purely emotional into the realm of the ideological. This question really has to do with how we perceive ourselves. Humanism, which purports to exalt man, denies the existence of the Creator, along with the idea that man is made in His image, and proclaims man to be merely a product of evolution and, therefore, takes a very indulgent view of murder. It has brought us to the point where we, as a nation, have indiscriminately killed millions of unborn babies since Roe v. Wade in 1973 while, at the same time, failing to rightfully execute those found guilty of committing monstrous crimes against their fellow human beings.

It should be clear that those who would follow Jesus have a responsibility to support government authorities in their God-given responsibilities to maintain law and order by punishing the evildoers. It should be just as clear that capital punishment is a part of the government's repertoire in dealing with these evildoers. Instead of making the government's work even harder by attempting to prohibit the death penalty, we should uphold the righteous hand of justice.[11]

I want to conclude this chapter with a statement made by Professor Ernest van den Haag in his interesting book, *Punishing Criminals*, a statement with which I agree wholeheartedly:

> A failure to terminate a murderer's life is not a celebration of human life, but exactly the opposite. Those who believe in the sacred right of an individual to live his life span uninterrupted by murder cannot

---

[11] See I Pet. 2:14; Tit. 3:1; Rom. 13:1-7.

affirm their devotion to that principle by dealing frivolously with those who violate it.

He went on to write:

The proposition is best understood by stretching it out on a graph in a demonstration of an [argument] *reductio ad absurdum*. A society that punishes a murderer by giving him a jail sentence of one week is a society that sets little store by human life. A society that holds human life so sacred that it is prepared to execute anyone who takes another human life, is a society that believes deeply in human life.

Chapter 12

The Closing Salvo

In concluding this study, I wish to make it clear that I believe that until, and unless, we are willing to make the logical projection of Biblical principles to their broadest applications in a society, we're not really communicating the gospel to that society at all. Although it is true that American culture has already been widely influenced by Biblical truths, nevertheless, in order for this to be done, it was necessary for certain Biblical principles to be "contextualized." By "contextualized," I mean a process that is defined as the application of Biblical truths to the circumstances and situations to be experienced in a particular (read "target") culture. For instance, it was necessary that the principle of the *master-slave* relationship articulated in the New Testament almost two thousand years ago be "contextualized" into the *employer-employee* relationship of our modern American society. Unfortunately, some who failed to do this believe the New Testament says nothing about our modern employer-employee environment. This, I think, is similar to the error pacifists make when they argue that the principles taught in Romans 13:1-7 are limited to the justice effected only by domestic law enforcement.

To properly understand the questions we have considered in this study, it is necessary to understand that Church (the kingdom of God) and State (civil government), although separate, were never intended to be mutually exclusive. Failing to understand this has caused some to believe Christians cannot scripturally function in both of these spheres at the same time. This was the position articulated by David Lipscomb in his book *Civil Government*. In it, Lipscomb repudiated any active participation in civil affairs, even to the point of not voting. He argued that human governments, owing their origin to man's rebellion against God, as he had wrongly concluded, were not proper spheres for Christian involvement. Although Romans 13:1-7 makes it clear that civil government is a creation of God, not man, Lipscomb's ideas were readily received by many Christians in the South after their devastating Civil War defeat. Raised in the South, and now having lived most of my life there, I am sorry to say that I have frequently been confronted with either Lipscomb's position or one of its modern-day variations. I say "sorry" because the Lipscomb position presents a totally unscriptural view of civil government that has caused churches of Christ, which are predominantly located in the South, to be without much impact in civil affairs.

Consequently, New Testament Christians, emerging from the difficulties of the 19th century and eschewing participation in civil government, as Lipscomb and others had influenced them to do, were much affected by the secularization that swept the 20th century. They bought into, nearly "lock, stock, and barrel," the secularization lie. In doing so, they gave themselves over to a traditional, uncritical and totally unscriptural view of the separation of Church (the sacred) and State (the secular). Yes, and as was previously pointed out, Christians do have an obligation to distinguish between the secular and the sacred; but it is just as true that we must never try to totally separate them, as Lipscomb thought. To do so would be to deny the Lordship of Jesus Christ over *all* of life—sacred and secular. Nevertheless, too many modern Christians have given themselves over to a view of Church and State that forces them to divide their lives into that which is sacred and that which is secular. This false dichotomy has forced an unscriptural compartmentalization of religion. Within the confines of an ever decreasing arena, New Testament Christians unashamedly proclaim belief in, and reliance upon, God; but outside these parameters—"cage" might be a better word—they have developed a reluctance to even mention His name.

So, although religion in the private sector may give the appearance of flourishing today, in the public arena it has been almost totally neutralized. As a result, Christianity may still be privately engaging to some, but it is socially irrelevant to most. The central sectors of society (business, technology, science, medicine, law, politics, *et cetera*) have been stripped of religious influence. As

Americans and, unfortunately, as Christians, we have thought it most proper to internalize our religion. This "privatization," or secret discipleship (i.e., the "Joseph of Arimathea Syndrome" of John 19:38), has added to the current secularization of America. But, more importantly, it has caused *true Christianity* (the kind we read about in the New Testament) to be without any real impact in public life. Afraid to mention the name of the Lord publicly—except within the limited confines of the local church and family—for fear of being thought of as un-American, uncivil, unprofessional, anti-social, sectarian, and fanatical, Christians now find themselves without any real impact in their communities. Instead of being the salt that savors and the light that shines out of darkness, as Matthew 5:13-16 requires, many of us have allowed the so-called "Wall" secularists erected between Church and State to force us to publicly blend in with the rest of society. And embarrassing as it all is, secularists became victors by default, in that they are occupying territory that we Christians have willingly, but mistakenly, withdrawn from. Thinking it our duty to espouse a principle that forces us to eliminate the Lord from *all* of government and *most* of society, we created the 20th century monster called "Secularism." Alive and well in the 21st century, this Frankenstein, which is now poised to destroy us, is an unnatural creation that should have never been created in the first place. In truth, we have been digging our own graves—conduct that has been aptly called "The Gravedigger Effect."

Seduced By A Metaphor

No student of the Bible would deny that Jesus taught there was to be a distinction between Church and State. During His earthly ministry, Jesus said: "Render therefore to Caesar the things that are Caesar's, and to God the things that are God's."[1] Even so, I feel confident the Lord never wanted His disciples to believe there was to be a separation of God and the State—that is to say, a

---

[1] Matt. 22:21.

complete divorcement of God-based morality from civil government. The "Wall," or in its more expanded form, "the wall of separation between Church and State," first articulated by Thomas Jefferson in a letter to the Danbury (Connecticut) Baptist Association, is a seductive metaphor that has subsequently misled many. The concept of an inseparable wall between Church and State, whether one believes it to have been taught by Jesus or espoused in the Constitution of the United States, surrenders to a simplistic understanding of a complicated subject. It is a gross hermeneutical error to use Matthew 22:21 as a proof-text for an absolute and inseparable wall between government and religion. Proof-texting or "Bumper Sticker Theology," as I prefer to call it, must give way to a conceptual or overall view of the Lord's teaching on any given subject. For example, the faith taught in John 3:16 cannot really be understood without the teaching found in James 2:14-26. Likewise, we would expect the truth taught in Matthew 22:21 to be amplified elsewhere in God's Word. And this is exactly what we find. In Titus 3:1, the Christian is taught to be "subject to rulers and authorities," which is just another way of saying, "Render therefore to Caesar the things that are Caesar's."

Those who have thought government to be absolutely autonomous and free from a God-based morality have failed to consider many Bible passages, including Colossians 2:10, where Jesus is said to be "the head of all principality and power." Not only is He "head over all things to the church," but He is "far above all principality and power and might and dominion, and every name that is named, not only in this age but also in that which is to come."[2] There is but one exception to the sovereignty of Jesus Christ, and this is the Father, "who put all things under Him."[3] As Christians, there is simply no excuse for not knowing what Nebuchadnezzar had to learn the hard way; namely, "the Most High rules in the kingdom of men."[4]

---

[2] Eph. 1:21-22.
[3] I Cor. 15:27.
[4] Dan. 4:25.

For the Christian to have believed that in order to honor Jesus Christ it was necessary for him to eliminate the Lord from *all* of government and *most* of society, is totally irreconcilable with the truths taught in the Bible. It is just such unquestioned allegiance to the erroneous doctrine of "the Wall" between Church and State that has caused churches of Christ to be without any appreciable impact on society and, as a result, very ineffective in their evangelistic efforts. Having rested our hopes on apologetics (the defense of a doctrine), we have sorely neglected discipleship (the living of a doctrine).[5]

In Matthew 5:13-16, Jesus taught us that we are to be the "salt" and "light" of the world. With but little thought given to the context, we can readily understand that the Lord was not referring to our "saying," but our "doing." Christians function as salt and light when others see our "good works and glorify (our) Father which is in heaven."

A world groping in darkness is benefited by the disciplined lives of a "chosen generation, a royal nation, a peculiar people."[6] So, when a Christian, who the Bible says, in Ephesians 2:10, has been created in Christ Jesus for good works is not living a godly life (i.e., is not actively doing Justice and Righteousness), he no longer can save himself from this "perverse generation,"[7] nor can he act so as to preserve this nation from God's righteous indignation.

Consequently, we should pray for, and seek to become, salty Christians who understand that although our Lord has returned to heaven, we are called upon to faithfully serve the *time*, *place* and *people* of a lost and dying world until that glorious day when, having been found faithful unto death,[8] we'll hear the One to whom we are betrothed say, "Well done my good and faithful servant."

As members of that great and glorious body of Christ, let us be determined to do justly, love mercy, and walk humbly with our

---

[5] See Gal. 2:20.
[6] I Pet. 2:9.
[7] Acts 2:40.
[8] See Rev. 2:10.

God as we serve our Families, our local Churches, our local, state and federal Governments, our Employers and Employees, and last of all, but certainly not least, our Neighbors. When we do so, we can be sure we are glorifying the One who purchased us with His own blood.

Index

www.ingramcontent.com/pod-product-compliance
Lightning Source LLC
Chambersburg PA
CBHW032052080426
42733CB00006B/248